In a
Dark Wood

In a Dark Wood

Personal Essays by Men on Middle Age

Edited by Steven Harvey

The University of Georgia Press
Athens and London

© 1996 by Steven Harvey

Published by the University of Georgia Press

Athens, Georgia 30602

All rights reserved

Designed by Betty Palmer McDaniel

Set in 10/14 Minion by Books International, Inc.

Printed and bound by Thomson-Shore, Inc.

The paper in this book meets the guidelines for
permanence and durability of the Committee
on Production Guidelines for Book Longevity
of the Council on Library Resources

Printed in the United States of America

00   99   98   97   96   C   5   4   3   2   1

00   99   98   97   96   P   5   4   3   2   1

Library of Congress Cataloging in Publication data

In a dark wood : personal essays by men on
middle age / edited by Steven Harvey.

   p.   cm.

  ISBN 0-8203-1846-9 (alk. paper)

  ISBN 0-8203-1878-7 (pbk.: alk. paper)

   1. Middle aged men—Psychology. 2. Middle
aged men—Attitudes.   I. Harvey, Steven, 1949 June 9–

HQ1090.I5   1996

305.24'4—dc20   95-52472

British Library Cataloging in Publication Data available

For my sons, Matt and Sam

In the middle of the journey of our life
I found myself in a dark wood
Where the straight way was lost.

DANTE

Contents

Acknowledgments

FRANKLIN BURROUGHS, "A Pastoral Occasion." Reprinted from *Billy Watson's Crocker Sack* by Franklin Burroughs, with permission of W. W. Norton. © 1991 by Franklin Burroughs. Originally published in the *Kenyon Review*.

BERNARD COOPER, "The Wind Did It." From *Maps to Anywhere* by Bernard Cooper. © 1990 by Bernard Cooper. Reprinted by permission of the University of Georgia Press.

GERALD EARLY, "Their Malcolm, My Problem." First published in *Harper's Magazine*. © 1992 by Gerald Early. Reprinted by permission of the author.

JOSEPH EPSTEIN, "An Older Dude." Reprinted from *Once More around the Block: Familiar Essays by Joseph Epstein*, with permission of W. W. Norton. © 1987 by Joseph Epstein.

STEVEN HARVEY, "Monogamy." From *A Geometry of Lilies: Life and Death in an American Family* by Steven Harvey. © 1993 by the University of South Carolina Press. Reprinted by permission of the University of South Carolina Press.

JAMES KILGO, "Inheritance of Horses." From *Inheritance of Horses* by James Kilgo. © 1994 by James Kilgo. Reprinted by permission of the University of Georgia Press.

SYDNEY LEA, "Honesty." From *Hunting the Whole Way Home.* © 1994 by the University Press of New England.

SAM PICKERING, "Selecting a Past." From *Still Life.* © 1990 by the University Press of New England.

SCOTT RUSSELL SANDERS, "Reasons of the Body." From *Secrets of the Universe* by Scott Russell Sanders. © 1991 by Scott Russell Sanders. Reprinted by permission of Beacon Press.

JOHN STONE, "Night Wanderings." First published in *The New York Times Magazine.* © 1992 by John Stone. Reprinted by permission of the author.

GEOFFREY WOLFF, "A Day at the Beach." From *A Day at the Beach* by Geoffrey Wolff. © 1992 by Geoffrey Wolff. Reprinted by permission of Alfred A. Knopf.

Introduction

An injured animal has a look in the eye that many middle-aged men understand—the look of a weakened and inarticulate creature. I have seen it in the eyes of wounded geese that my dad would mercifully kill, snapping their long necks with a twist of his hand, and though I've never hunted deer, I can imagine doe eyes and that helpless, plaintive gaze just before the animal is put away with a blow, a blast, or a bloody slit. Men who enact these deadly mercies know the look because they have worn it in corridors, in the gym, or on the streets—wherever they are sized up and judged—and once youth is behind them many see it each morning in their own mirrors.

Unprepared in their youth for intimacy, and notoriously bad at expressing feelings, men move through a chattering world silent about fears and longings. This is the cliché, isn't it?—but one with the ring of truth. In the teenage boy's world of muscle and sports, the language of introspection has little place. From the serenity of the deer stand or the exile of left field to the agony of a blind date, the American male passes through much of his youth with little to say. *Poker-faced, stoic, strong and silent*—these are the ideal characteristics a boy emulates on the way to becoming a man of few words.

As men move into positions of authority, this masculine silence usually deepens. With age they have more to hide and less to say, especially about their weaknesses. Power, always an issue in the background of a boy's life, is suddenly shoved forward and all of the attributes that might gentle the beast that drives adulthood—humor, courtesy, and conversation—are enlisted to consolidate a powerful position. Admissions of weakness and other expressions of vulnerability—the gateway to the honest expression of emotions—is rarely an option for adult men.

"Ask him," the women in my life would say if I harbored an unanswered personal question for my father.

"What's to say?" he usually replied when I finally got the courage to ask—his instinctive response—followed by a mumbled "let's see," as he looked ahead into his answer, deciding what to leave out.

The silence can be broken—a meeting of minds and hearts—but only after the demands of the body have been met, the handshake coming before the words. Some men, like the souls at the fosse in Homer's hell, require blood before they can talk—a fight or a hunt—as James Kilgo's essays about hunting and the stories men tell afterward suggest. For many, like Scott Russell Sanders, sports is a language of the body, a physical dialogue between fathers and sons. Much of the time, though, men are imprisoned by silence, awash in emotions and at a loss for words. You can see it in their eyes.

The silence of middle-aged men on the subject of their feelings is the reason for this book. As it turns out, a few good men are articulate about their emotions, giving voice to anxieties in beautifully written testimonies that are sad and funny by turns and, at times, wise. They are the writers of the personal essay, a form perfectly suited to the task.

Phillip Lopate, in the introduction to *The Art of the Personal Essay,* calls the essay "the voice of middle age" and the point of view it offers as "the fruit of ripened experience." The form gives middle-aged men

plenty of room to tell their stories. Franklin Burroughs takes his dog
to the vet for a lethal injection; Geoffrey Wolff barely survives care at a
hospital in the Caribbean; and Bernard Cooper's father heads for
Samoa to get a new lease on life. These tales need to be told, and in the
telling the essayist raids the costume shop of fiction, trying on techniques that novelists use to make narrations vivid: imagery, dialogue,
suggestive settings, plot complications, climax. Themes are embodied
in such techniques, the word made flesh, and a first step is taken toward telling the truth.

Unlike fiction writers, though, essayists feel free to go beyond story
to state ideas—or at least mull them over, weighing possibilities, considering contradictions, toying with ambiguities. In telling their tales
they create a voice that we trust, reliable not because it gets the facts
right or for that matter the ideas, but because it sheds irony and be-
lieves in itself. "Put that way, I see your point," the successful essay
allows us to admit, voice bridging incidents and ideas to become a
powerful tool for presenting—and sharing—all that we tend to keep to
ourselves. Such honesty, as Sydney Lea writes in his essay, is "enabling."
Here flesh is made word, though never the last word, the meaning of
an incident explored as it is presented, the writer inching toward
wisdom. It is a way of giving voice to the anxiety in those eyes.

So what kind of voice do these middle-aged writers bring to their joys
and woes? What strategies do they enlist on the way to an enabling
honesty? First of all, most of them are funny. "I am fifty," writes Joseph
Epstein, "and, realist that I am, I must now conclude that my life is at
least a third over." "Let me just say," Geoffrey Wolff writes as he con-
templates heart surgery and his debts, "that as difficult as it would have
been for pals and kin to walk this planet without me, it would have
been catastrophic for Visa and Diners' Club." And John Stone quotes

"W. H. Auden's definition of a professor as 'one who talks in someone else's sleep.'"

Sometimes the jokes are one-liners, like these. Most of the time, though, the humor runs over the course of a paragraph or through the whole piece and cannot be removed from context. Burroughs's description of his old dog as a debauched roué passionately pursuing a young bitch that has spent the day rolling in rotten fish is one example. So is the section in Sanders's essay about his father who, as a young man, picks a bar fight with a man who turns out to be a college boxing coach. In the course of the paragraph he is flattened, but wins a scholarship and a spot on the team nonetheless.

Most of this humor is self-deprecating, designed to relieve self-pity. Behind the joke is an anxiety—about age, sex, change, or failure—that is eased by laughter. So, Geoffrey Wolff, after his heart attack, began to compile "an omnium-gatherum of clichés" involving death and the heart such as "You'd die to see her" or "You're all heart." These darker sentiments are the flip side of the humor, and occasionally, when the joking stops and the speaker feels trapped, the baldly stated misery pokes through. "So here I am," groans Gerald Early, a middle-class, middle-aged black man, "caught between my daughters, who find my race lessons tiresome, and my students, who think me somehow insufficiently black." In short, the "thinking life" has its liabilities: "The truth is," Lopate says, "most wisdom is embittering."

But such whining is rare, and seldom the final comment. Swept beneath the rug by a joke or two, these complaints usually stay hidden below the surface, smoothed down by the soft shoe of an assured prose style, what Lopate calls the "unnerving calm" and "stoical balance of middle age." Despite occasional, pitiful outbursts, the essay must go on—using wit, style, and freshness to hide any lumps. It is easy to be cynical about this, to weary of a voice that, like the voices of airline pilots, keeps calm on the brink of despair—but there is good reason for it. Such a voice buys the writer time to find meaning in all that seems arbitrary.

This quest for meaning explains why the essayists in this collection are so fond of making lists, a preoccupation, I suspect, of those who are beyond youth. Epstein writes about schedules. Burroughs keeps a tally of every bird his dog retrieved. Pickering makes a list of the contents of a spice box that says more about him than he is willing at first to admit. Best of all is the list, in Bernard Cooper's essay, of things—a pile of coupons, ads, and love notes—on the dining room table, the "makeshift desk" where his father eats lunch and checks his mail, that define the man. Such lists—an accounting like this—is a way to beat back disillusionment, the naming and noting preliminary to the shaping that brings meaning.

And meaning is the business and preoccupation of these essays—the urge to bring the ingredients of life to a boil. A few essayists offer a recipe, tentative answers to their questions. So Gerald Early reaches a momentary stay against his own confusion by arguing that Afro-Americans, despite the hyphenated, dual identity that they cannot shed, are first Americans, bequeathing his old mentor Malcolm X to another confused generation. Most of the essays, though, have no solutions, the curled lists on the table offering tantalizing hints but never adding up. Like the game show *Jeopardy* that Cooper's father watches, the answers in these essays are questions. "Jeez this game is tough," the dad says, frustrated at not knowing the right response while watching the show. Later, he massages his son's back, "calling questions into the night," the moment of words and flesh a metaphor for what these essays do.

"Middle-aged," Epstein writes, "the English language contains jollier words, surely." It also has more precise ones. Society offers a legal age for the end of childhood and a specific age for retirement discounts at motels, but no clear definition of middle age exists. One of the reasons it is so hard to define is that it is, as the name suggests, transitional, and well upon most of us before we know it is happening. "You don't recall having booked passage," Epstein writes, "but you appear to be, very slowly, sailing to Byzantium." It probably is best defined not as a time, but as a set of preoccupations—the kind that these writers address in questions called into the dark.

It is a time of life that is preoccupied with time itself. "The minutes, the hours, the days go as slowly as ever; it is those damn weeks, months, and years that now speed past," Epstein writes. Like the bald professor with a toupee and a coed under his arm, these writers have trouble resisting the urge to tinker with the clock. Pickering, anxious about the future, decides with Quixotic boldness and humbling results to pick a new past for himself. Sydney Lea's essay begins with a time capsule, an attempt to capture a past, which, when he cannot find the capsule ten years later, serves as a reminder that, despite memory and souvenirs, we cannot hold onto the past any more than we can change it.

There is the constant hunt for true measures in life. Like the doorjamb marking in ticks the heights of our children, all that does not change becomes such a measuring device. Gerald Early rereads Malcolm X's autobiography and seeing the familiar text with new eyes knows that he has let go of ideas that once were cherished by him but now no longer ring true, indicating the ways in which time has worked on him. The games—basketball and baseball—that Sanders plays with his son mark the passing of generations more accurately than the calendar and reveal where Sanders himself falls in the scheme of things.

By the same token, every change is a marker, often a memento mori, including the obsessive concern with health that Cooper and his father cannot avoid: "Burning at the center of our discourse like the sun is the one subject we never miss, the subject which dwarfs and out-shines all others: the state of our health." Burroughs, putting his dog to sleep, frames the problem this way: "Even if it is only your canine or feline proxy, and not yourself, you do not like to be reminded that some patients enter hospitals for the purpose of dying." The body, these essays remind us, is a teacher. Stone follows it blindly when sleepwalking, which he sees as "attempts to do what can't be done in the light," the body acting on yearnings we have denied.

Work, oddly enough, does not enter into the discussion much. The disciplines of work life have become second nature, habits to be assumed and ignored. Whether they enjoy their jobs or not, most middle-aged men are good at what they do, which brings some measure of satisfaction. As Epstein puts it, "you begin to get the feeling that you are playing, as the sports announcers say, 'in control.'" Middle-aged men still hold most of the positions of power in our culture, after all, a fact usually delivered as an accusation, and are often admired and envied—at times emulated—by the young. So successes and failures at work, enjoyed and endured by this time, are largely seen for what they are: a subset of the larger issue of human relationships.

At the same time, there is little patience for ideology. None of these writers, when writing about middle age, are inclined to discuss the pros and cons of any -*ism*. There are no manifestoes for socialism, here, and little soul searching about feminism, either. Age has led these men, regardless of past allegiances, to a pragmatic view of life. Gerald Early, for instance, no longer sees youthful fascination with Afro-centrism as a worthy ideal but as a typically American form of ro-manticizing, one that is exciting, but ultimately as unsatisfactory for black Americans as the model of Gatsby, in F. Scott Fitzgerald's novel, is for whites. These middle-aged writers simply cannot muster much interest in public causes and are unwilling to measure themselves against the lofty standards of youthful ideals, preferring, instead, to stand as tall as they can in the mere reality of their own homes.

In fact, the most telling measure of middle age involves encounters of men with the young, especially their own children. According to Epstein, these meetings are the surest indicators of a man's status. "However young one may feel, one is no longer young when in the eyes of the young one is not young." Playing catch, Sanders sees that his throws fall short of his son's, his weary arm delivering the bad news to him as his boy keeps backing up, and Early feels the gap in his daughters' lukewarm response to his tale of youthful heroism. These encounters are often the moment of truth for the writer, but rarely are they a source of bitterness. The young are our future, and all of us have a stake in them, a realization grudgingly accepted.

At the other end of the spectrum, encounters with fathers measure and define the writers, too. Middle age does, after all, put these men squarely between parents and children, making them oddly aware, by comparison, of the whole span of life. They can't help but see that life goes through stages, and different as they are from those ahead and behind they recognize that all who live long enough must pass through each stage. So there is much poignancy in these meetings with fathers, and a sense of the uncanny, too, the middle-aged writer seeing himself mysteriously represented in the older man. We are all in this mess together, the encounters with dads remind us. "My father awoke," Cooper writes, remembering a dream about visiting his father's bedroom. "'Dad,' I whispered, 'are we getting older?' 'Here,' he said, lifting the blanket. 'Here,' he said, patting the bed."

And women? They probably bear the brunt of middle-aged, male anxiety, whether the men love them, leave them, or get left behind. "You live," Epstein remarks, "and you yearn." A few men are mercifully unaffected by new yearnings, feeling no tension between their lot in life and their desires. In an essay entitled "These Essays, My Life," Pickering is appropriately prosaic about his desires. "As for my love calls," he writes, "I'm the sort of fellow who gargles once or twice a week before going to bed, then a bit later puts his book down, raises himself on his elbows and turning to his mate says, 'How about it, old girl?'"

Most middle-aged men, though, sense a strain seeing new life all about them—the fecundity of the young—and feeling left out. Schools of fish, suggestive of the seminal rush, are the symbol of this in our poetry: Robert Lowell's famous "chinook salmon jumping and falling back" and Yeats's "mackerel-crowded sea" suggesting all that the aging man, a "tattered coat upon a stick," must let go of. Burroughs in his essay associates the annual summertime bounty of menhaden in his river with youth.

James Kilgo's essay gives an achingly vivid portrait of the kind of havoc that this middle-aged sexual hunger can inflict on married life—the familiar story of the love affair that destroys a marriage. In it he tells the tale of his grandfather's infidelity, a tale he pieces together out of memory, letters, and speculations. "What I don't know—cannot imagine—is how the whole thing started," the naive grandson in Kilgo writes, but soon the writer in him comes up with the familiar scenario: an opportunity (a peaceful cabin by a millpond), a motive (depression, the death of a father), and a scene of the crime (a room with a Victrola and a stack of RCA records with red labels). Once his grandfather was found out, the consequences were swift—a marriage of separate bedrooms. This is a grandson's tale, but despite changed mores and the distance in time (the more common outcome now would be divorce), the story rings true and claims us, names us, just as it does Kilgo who inherited his grandfather's name.

At times, the sexual hunger is homoerotic—another potent reminder of the power of sexual passion in the lives of middle-aged men.

Sydney Lea's memory of the smile of a hunting companion is sensuous and loving: "I could not see the man's big grin," he recalls, "but I remember somehow *feeling* it like the sudden breeze that kicked up, bending the marshweeds one way, ferrying the smell to us of the heath, a rankness I still inhale like perfume." And Kilgo's grandfather, locked out of his marriage, survives emotionally by writing love letters—that's what Kilgo calls them—to a lifelong male friend, his college roommate, the yearning for flesh sublimated in words: "I have had things that wracked me," he writes, in one letter, "but somehow I always felt better when I had shared them with you."

For most of these essayists, though, sexual passion—blatant or disguised—is not an end, but a beginning, a door opening on a variety of relationships, and they have found that over time and often through children, sexual hunger has been transformed into the urge to nurture—something akin to a feminine paternity. Certainly nurture is the guiding emotion of the essays by Pickering, Stone, and Burroughs. What we have here is the traditional male role of protector made suddenly androgynous, and human, by the realization, which comes with age, that nothing can be protected forever and little can be protected for long. Burroughs, hoping to shelter his children from grief over the dog the family would kill, is fully aware that the lessons in grief that the death of an animal teaches are complex. Considering each child, from youngest to oldest, he writes: "Hannah's would be Eden-grief—natural tears easily shed, and soon wiped. Elizabeth would know more, and Coles yet more, of the pretense that infects even our most spontaneous sorrows." A father can protect from grief, but from such pretense—from such lost innocence—what protection?

Pickering is only half joking when he says he wants to protect his children from becoming like himself. He plays the bumbler in his essays, so that the kids will feel superior to him and be freed, he tells us tongue-in-cheek from living in his paternal shadow, "endlessly measuring themselves against steep, high standards." Letting the children be themselves is the grandest kind of nurture, a trick no father can do with complete success, though he can soften the blow: "To some extent," Pickering writes, "I am selecting pasts for them, pasts, I hope though, of mood not abilities, pasts soft and gentle and smiling." Perhaps the old saw about men and women becoming more alike as they get older has some redeeming truth to it. It seems, at any rate, to offer a way out of some of the anxieties of middle age.

Death is not explicitly discussed in many of these essays, but like a skull, it is there in each of them, just beneath the surface. Lea's thoughts about the time capsule he buried are mixed with memories of a dead friend. Cooper's father seeks answers to his questions about death by reading about Aztec ruins. And Burroughs buries his dog.

"It is not always easy to distinguish between the love of life and the fear of death," Epstein writes, wary of being absorbed by thoughts of death. Burroughs is repulsed by the fate of his old dog that can do nothing but eat: "It is somehow obscene, too much like the cold vision of Death as a skeleton whose hunger is never glutted, or a parody of all the unseemly desires that stay with us, long after we should have satisfied or subdued them." The temptation to substitute merely being alive for living is one of death's dangerous lessons.

But mortality is a great teacher, as well, because of lessons it offers in life's limits. By middle age most of these writers—despite failures and unmet desires—have come to accept who they are by learning to live with what they will never be. "I believe I have come to grips with the distinct possibility that I will never be a United States senator, or own a horse in the Kentucky Derby, or write a novel as long and as good as Proust's," Epstein writes. "I can live with these deprivations. I don't want your pity."

Once accepted, this awareness of limits is liberating. It allows Lea to admit that even if he will never be able to give an accurate record of his life he still feels the need to continue the attempt. Each stage of life, Sanders realizes, must be lived for what it has to offer: "I mean to live the present year before rushing off to any future ones." And recognizing limits leads Pickering to understand that his plans to protect his children from himself are in vain—no one has that much control over his own life, not to mention the life of another.

At this point these essays come close to wisdom—"perspective," as Epstein calls it. "Things that used to outrage you can now sometimes amuse you. You do not expect so much from other people, or from yourself." In short, "Baggier and saggier though your skin may grow, you feel more comfortable in it." If there is fear in the eyes of the wounded doe just before the kill, there is often a calm, as well, a recognition of the futility of struggle in the face of the inevitable. That is the final lesson of these essayists who regularly face the mirror of the blank page and have found a way to live with the image they see there.

STEVEN HARVEY

An Older Dude

JOSEPH EPSTEIN

JOSEPH EPSTEIN is the editor of the *American Scholar* and a professor of literature and writing at Northwestern University. His books of essays include *The Middle of My Tether* (1987), *Once More around the Block* (1990), and *Line Out for a Walk* (1991), all published by Norton. He was also the editor for *Best American Essays, 1993*.

Five-o, roman numeral L. Half a century. Five big ones, baby. I refer to my age. This year I turn fifty, with no hope of turning back. It is a bit of an amazement to me. Him Tarzan, me boy, or so I used to think, except that now I am decades older than the inarticulate ape-man himself and a good deal less agile even than Jane. I, a stripling, a mere lad, only yesterday a fine broth of a boy, shall soon have fifty winters under my belt. The evidence for my age is there. I look in the mirror and, like an actor in a long-running play, I know my lines; also my wrinkles, pouches, and circles. Recently, filling out a bureaucratic form, I was able to supply my birth date, height, weight, and eye color readily enough, but when asked the color of my hair I instinctively lifted my cap to let the clerk decide for herself on brown or gray. On a good day, when the light is right, I do not look a week over forty-eight, though where I live there are not that many good days. But enough of these little self-deceptions. I am fifty, and, realist that I am, I must now conclude that my life is at least a third over.

St. Augustine says that "we should not underestimate the significance of number, since in many passages of sacred scripture numbers have meaning for the conscientious interpreter." In my own life, I have paid little attention to the number of my years. The supposedly great decade markers—twenty, thirty, forty—whirred past, and I paid them no more heed than as a boy I did to the Burma-Shave signs along the highway: I noted them, smiled, and drove on. Owing perhaps to my having become a father fairly young—I had charge of four sons by the age of twenty-six—I was unable to linger overlong on the glories of youth, except in fantasy. I tended to be precocious in other, less important ways. Perhaps it was the era into which I was born, but I never looked upon youth as an occupation or religion or social class. It was instead something one enjoyed—if one was lucky—while passing through it.

"Act your age," mothers would say to their children when I was a boy. "Be a man," fathers would exhort their sons. "Aw, grow up," older sisters and teenage girl friends would exclaim. In fact, growing up didn't seem like a bad idea. A goodly number of grown-ups walked the streets in those days. Think only of the movies. Edward G. Robinson, Humphrey Bogart, Cary Grant, James Cagney—these were men who appeared on screen in suits and ties, hats, black shoes. Grown-ups. Robert Redford, Dustin Hoffman, Robert De Niro, Harrison Ford— these are men who, at the same age as Robinson, Bogart & Co., one thinks of as characteristically in jeans, sneakers or boots, loose collars. Graduate students. One could make a similar comparison of actresses. Compare Bette Davis and Jane Fonda, Ingrid Bergman and Meryl Streep. All are fine actresses, but the former are women, the latter girls who continue to grow older. Nowadays there aren't so many grown-ups—just a lot of older dudes. It is, apparently, what the culture calls for just now. I happen to be writing this in a short-sleeve rugby shirt, chino pants, and tasseled loafers. I'm an older dude myself.

Just as I have never been able to think of Hugh Hefner as a playboy— he has always looked to me like an insurance salesman—so neither can I quite think of myself as an older dude, all physical evidence to the contrary notwithstanding. Not that I wish to remain forever young. Unlike Philip Larkin, who once declared that not having to get mixed up with children more than compensated for having to start earning a living, I rather enjoyed my childhood and adolescence. But enough was enough. Becoming grown-up, with its promise of freedom, was always more alluring to me than anything youth could promise. The allure was there when I was very young. At the age of seven, at most eight, I used to watch a man named Sid Carter play softball in my neighborhood, and he represented, at least for me, some of the promise of growing up. Sid Carter must have been only in his early twenties, but from the perspective of age seven or eight that was plenty old. A marvelous athlete, he could hit a softball from Farwell Beach in Chicago roughly to Bessarabia. Tall, slender, tanned, his sandy-colored hair brushed straight back, he was dapper even in softball duds. In street clothes he was never less than perfectly turned out; elegance and flair came naturally to him. He drove a cream-colored Plymouth convertible. I recall thinking that, when I grew up, I, too, would own a convertible.

I never have. I suppose I never shall. My eldest son does, though. Not long ago he traded in his car for a high-powered British sports car. He called to report this to me, with what I sensed was a slight trepidation in his voice lest his square old man think him frivolous. "Dear boy," I said, "I'm glad that you have a sports car. I want you to have all the things I never had: sports cars, a beautiful Chinese girl friend, lots of foreign languages." If you sense some yearning here, you are probably correct. If you sense serious regret, you are mistaken. I shall muddle through all right if I never drive down the Pacific Highway, the top down on my Porsche, gently teasing the lovely Dai-yu in Persian. Yet growing older does remind one of all the things one is now unlikely to do, or have, or be. I believe I have come to grips with the distinct possibility that I will never be a United States senator, or own a horse in the Kentucky Derby, or write a novel as long and as good as Proust's. I can live with these deprivations. I don't want your pity.

What I would prefer is that you find a way to stop the clock from running. When one is young, one lives as if one had a thousand years to go. Once one hits fifty, as E. B. White, a considerable hypochondriac, once said, one feels one has about twenty minutes to live. One is humming the damn "September Song" all the time. In this morning's paper I read that Robert A. Comfort, one of the five men who robbed the Hotel Pierre in 1972, died at age fifty-three. Alexis de Tocqueville—Mr. T. himself—was taken out of the game at the same age. Philip Larkin, a man who seemed to have had the gift of perpetual middle age, while in his fifties (he died at sixty-three) once remarked: "If you assume you're going to live to be seventy, seven decades, and think of each decade as a day of the week, starting with Sunday, then I'm on Friday afternoon now. Rather a shock, isn't it?" It is. It also forces one to place a whole new interpretation on the notion of T.G.I.F.

As I turn fifty, it occurs to me that, unlike Tocqueville or Robert A. Comfort, I shall never write a great book or take part in an adventure such as a three-million-dollar heist. Neither shall I slam dunk a basketball nor publish a translation of Horace. Some of these things are technically possible—the robbery and the Latin translation—but more and more unlikely. I recently met a man who all his life wished to fly a plane; at sixty-four, upon his retirement, he learned to do so; and now, nearing seventy, he is about to fly solo to Europe. Impressive. I should love to learn to play the harpsichord, and with the injection of large sums of money in lessons and even larger sums of time given over to practice, my guess is that I could learn to play "Clair de lune" with a proficiency that, should a person with good manners be listening to me, would doubtless bring on in him a hemorrhage owing to violently suppressed laughter. But I am certain not to attempt to learn to play the harpsichord. There are too many other items on my agenda that are more pressing. Reaching the age of fifty may not confer wisdom—that honorary degree is given to few and never at commencement time—but it does allow one to understand rather better the poet Joseph Brodsky's remark that "every choice is essentially a flight from freedom."

The fact is that I am a man on a schedule. Some people are and some people aren't on a schedule, and the people who aren't are probably luckier. Those people who are on a schedule—who plan to be millionaires by the age of thirty, publish ten books by the age of forty, or hold serious economic or political power by the age of fifty—always hear the clock ticking, feel the light breeze caused by the turning of calendar pages, sense footsteps (whose?) following them. My own schedule is far from clear, though in some loose way I have always kept one. Its chief purpose appears to be to convince me that I am, inevitably, a bit behind. In college, not long after I somewhat inchoately decided I should like to become a writer, I met a classmate who, at the age of sixteen, had already published a short story in *New World Writing,* a magazine with a paperback book format that included among its contributors Federico García Lorca, William Carlos Williams, and Ignazio Silone. Not yet out of the starting gate, I already felt myself several furlongs off the pace. Henceforth I carefully noted the birth dates of published writers younger than I, and while I did not wish them ill, I did hope they would slow down.

My classmate who published a story in *New World Writing* at sixteen has not, so far as I know, published anything since. What happened to him? Having opened so grandly, did he then draw bad cards: a fatal illness, an automobile accident, alcoholism? Or did he instead forego life lived on a schedule? Did he come across the advice of Lambert

Strether? In Henry James's *The Ambassadors,* Lambert Strether tells the character little Bilham, "Live all you can; it's a mistake not to. It doesn't matter so much what you do in particular, so long as you have your life." When issuing that sound advice, Strether was fifty-five, or five years older than I—and Henry James, when putting the advice in Strether's mouth, was himself fifty-eight. Good advice though it is, is it available to one who is on a schedule? The question is, of course, one that occurred to Henry James—what serious question didn't?—for James himself was on a schedule, piling up book after book, so that in later years he wondered if he had allowed himself to live as fully as he might have done. As Strether goes on to tell little Bilham, "Still, one has the illusion of freedom; therefore don't be, like me, without the memory of that illusion. I was either, at the right time, too stupid or too intelligent to have it; I don't quite know which. Of course, at present, I'm a case of reaction against the mistake; and the voice of re-action should, no doubt, as always be taken with an allowance."

The only other American writer as good on the subject of middle age as Henry James is that great klutzy genius Theodore Dreiser. After Dreiser lost a decade of his writing life to a mental collapse and to re-gaining his confidence following the failure of *Sister Carrie,* he wrote like a man on a very strict if often confused schedule. Dreiser created the most powerful portraits of middle-aged men in American liter-ature: Lester Kane in *Jennie Gerhardt,* Frank Cowperwood in the so-called *Trilogy of Desire,* and, most memorably, George Hurstwood in *Sister Carrie.* What is astonishing is that Dreiser created Hurstwood, the quintessence of the middle-aged man in crisis, while he, Dreiser, was still in his twenties. It was Dreiser who, in Hurstwood, depicted the mid-life crisis fully seventy years before it became a cliché in the thick-fingered hands of the popular psychologists, thus confirming Freud's famous statement that psychology has most to learn from the poets.

I am pleased to report that I myself have not yet had anything resembling a mid-life crisis, at least as such episodes are advertised in popular culture, and I plan to go to my grave without one. Merely because the label is there doesn't mean everyone has to paste it upon his forehead. Besides, with the span of life increasing, it is no longer quite so clear where mid-life is. *Life Begins at Forty* was the title of Walter B. Pitkin's bestseller of 1932, a book written in cheerful reaction to the then-prevailing notion that senescence first began to set in at forty. Nowadays it more often seems that not life but adulthood begins at forty—sometimes between obtaining an MBA and acquiring a condominium. A great deal in contemporary culture permits one to indulge the delusion that one is still youthful well into one's thirties and even one's forties.

The moment of truth will arrive. However young one may feel, one is no longer young when in the eyes of the young one is not young. Somerset Maugham tells, in *A Writer's Notebook,* that the moment of truth came for him when, one day in his early forties, he got into a cab with a woman and her niece, and the niece took the strapontin, or tip seat, leaving the more comfortable seats for her aunt and him. (If you can recall tip seats in cabs, you are no longer so young yourself, darling.) A bachelor friend of mine noted that the moment of truth came for him when a younger woman he was out with suggested that they repair to a bar that had "a really knock-out sound system." Another friend marked the moment when, after a day spent outdoors, he returned home to discover that, owing to thinning hair, the top of his head was sunburned. My own moment came when, delivering a lecture on Theodore Dreiser to a class of college freshmen, I began by saying that "Dreiser was the first major American writer from the other side of the tracks." No sooner was the sentence out of my mouth than it occurred to me that my class could have no notion about what tracks I was talking about. I was thirty-seven, and obviously old well before my time.

My time was part of the problem. I was born in 1937, which means that in 1965 I was twenty-eight years old. I mention 1965 because that was the year that the era known—with chronological inexactitude—as the "sixties" got under way in earnest, with the prominence of the Free Speech Movement at the University of California in Berkeley. Virginia Woolf famously (and rather dubiously) declared that human nature changed in 1910; I am quite certain that human nature did not change in 1965 either, but one of the things that did begin to change in that year was the way people thought about age. Suddenly, to be young was everything, and even not very young people became aggressively, even militantly, youthful. The ground for the apotheosis of youth was pre-pared by the election of John F. Kennedy and the orgy of publicity given our young president and his youthful staff. By the middle 1960s this apotheosis of youth had taken a rivalrous, slightly nasty turn. Old geezers among us will recall one of many slogans of the day: "Don't trust anyone over thirty."

I was not yet thirty, and hence technically trustworthy, but exceed-ingly ill-prepared to join the kiddie corps. I had a family and a well-paying job; I had, for crying out loud, a mortgage. Wearing my hair in the style of George Eliot or pulled back in a ponytail like Debbie Reynolds did not seem to be, as people said at the time, "my thing." I prefer to think that I had too much irony—and, I hope, iron—in my makeup to smoke pot with either a straight or a laughing face. I rather liked to wear a necktie; had I wished to wear bell-bottoms, I should have joined the Navy. Allen Ginsberg was not my idea of a serious writer, nor Timothy Leary of a clear thinker, nor Herbert Marcuse of a profound philosopher. The sixties, when you got right down to it, was not my idea of a nice time.

With the arrival of the sixties it was as if a curtain—I believe a man named Churchill has already used up the metaphor of an "iron curtain"—had descended that divided the young from those who chose not to be young. Age had less to do with it than temperament and condition: John Lennon, the head Beatle, for example, was only three years younger than I and a year or two older than George Will, the conservative columnist and a grown-up. Natural predilections of temperament put me on the side of the not-young—E. T. A. Hoffmann, not Abbie Hoffman, was my idea of a hero—but, temperament aside, having a family clinched it. Experiments with high-powered drugs of the kind that went on in the sixties may have been interesting, but psychological interest was not the first thing to come to mind when I learned that a friend of my adolescent step-son had killed himself with an overdose of LSD. The sexual freedom of the sixties was also enticing, but, such are the limitations of human nature, it, too, did not come without cost. If I found myself on the not-young side of the curtain, others my age and older chose the young side, and many of them have remained there, living out their days as post-hippie Dorian Grays.

At fifty you can no longer claim that you are young, the way you might, say, at forty-five, and get away with it. At fifty, however young, even immature, you may feel, you have to begin regarding yourself as middle-aged, early middle-aged, if that adjective makes you feel any better, but middle-aged nonetheless. At fifty you can look much younger than you are. If that is important to you (and if it was not important to lots of people, health clubs and plastic surgeons would be out of business). At fifty you can, with training, run a marathon, play serious tennis, swim the English Channel. At fifty, again with training, you can have a lover of twenty-four. (I once knew a man in his early fifties who was married to a woman of twenty-three, but this same man also kept a mistress of forty-five. When I remarked on this un-usual reversal of procedure, and asked him why, with so young a wife, he needed an older mistress, he put out his hands, palms to the heav-ens, and replied that he had to have someone to talk to.) At fifty you can still be in pretty good shape—*for fifty.*

Middle-aged—the English language contains jollier words, surely. Middle-aged has something of the ring of the end of the party about it. It suggests loss of hair and gains in flesh, stiffening of joints and loosening of teeth; it suggests a dimming of vision and memory, of physical and mental powers generally. It is a Bosporus, a golden Horn, of the life span, where not east and west but age and youth meet; and like Istanbul, the city on the banks of the Bosporus, middle age can be filled with not always charming surprises: you make it through fewer and fewer nights without arising to inspect the plumbing; in winter the hair departs your shins; the clerk at the hardware store, with irony you could live without, refers to you as "young feller"; you cannot remember what you had for dinner on Tuesday, but you can remem-ber the lyrics to Vaughan Monroe's hit songs. You don't recall having booked passage, but you appear to be, very slowly, sailing to Byzan-tium, which, as Yeats seems to imply, is the country of timelessness.

On the positive side, at fifty, if life has been kind, leaving you with no serious illnesses or permanent disappointments, you begin to get the feeling that you are playing, as the sports announcers say, "in control." You see more going on around you. Setbacks are easier to take; victo-ries are no less pleasant, but you know that the sweet taste they bring does not last long. Baggier and saggier though your skin may grow, you feel more comfortable in it. Things that used to outrage you can now sometimes amuse you. You do not expect so much from other people, or from yourself. You care less about what other people think of you. This last point is similar to one made by Somerset Maugham, who was always a rigorous registrar of his own age. In *A Writer's Notebook* Maugham wrote: "That is what makes youth unhappy, the vehement anxiety to be like other people, and that is what makes middle age tolerable, the reconciliation with oneself." I hesitate to use the word, lest I be thought to be claiming it for myself, but middle age does sometimes give one the faintest suggestion that one may be acquiring "perspective."

Yet is it perspective that explains what I can only describe as my loss of awe for the living? When I was younger, it seemed that giants walked the earth: Churchill, Gandhi, de Gaulle in politics; Matisse, Stravinsky, Thomas Mann in art; Einstein, Fermi, Planck in science. The last figure for whom I felt a similar reverence was George Balanchine. The only living figure for whom I feel anything approaching such regard is Solzhenitsyn. Still, I wonder: Have I grown larger, smarter, surer in my perspective, or have men and women grown smaller in some indefinable way? I continue to respect what I take to be solid achievement in art and scholarship, but age has brought with it a loss of the capacity for adulation.

It was Evelyn Waugh who, having submitted himself to a painful and less than altogether necessary operation for hemorrhoids, claimed that his motive for doing so was perfectionism. I cannot claim to have had any serious standing as a perfectionist, but, now at middle age, any tendency in that direction has departed (gone perhaps to the same place to which the hair on my shins departs in winter). I am also through with self-improvement programs. But I do note around my apartment the presence of a plastic jump rope, two ten-pound barbells, and racquetball equipment—all there to testify to my hopes for one day getting into shape. What shape? At fifty, I suppose an oval is most likely. Intellectual self-improvement programs, too, are over for me. All I wish now is to become a little less stupid in the years left and to become more than a little better at my craft. As people close to me will tell you, I was never much good at self-improvement anyway.

From the perspective of fifty, I can now see that I have been extremely lucky. Lucky not to have been seriously ill, lucky to have been born in an interesting and free country, lucky even in my generation. Mine has been a generation that has missed having to go to war, which, in the present century, is like having lived out of doors in the rain and somehow avoided getting wet. My generation was much too young for World War II, still too young for Korea, and then too old for Vietnam. Having come of age in the United States in the 1950s, we missed the excitement of generations that came of age before ours—excitement, however, that carried certain penalties with it. The twenties, for example, when Prohibition was in force, produced an inordinately large number of alcoholics, largely because, as a man of that generation once explained it to me, drinking was inseparable from the idea of the illicit, and hence inseparable, too, from excitement. The thirties, with its crunching Depression, left a great many people hostage to anxiety over money all their lives, while a great many other people lapsed into the swamp of sectarian politics, from which they, too, never quite re-emerged. To have come of age in the forties was to have one's maturity marked indelibly by World War II. But to have come of age in the fifties was to miss being swamped by public events, to be a little out of it, and, when you came right down to it, to be a little out of it was not a bad place to be. To be absolutely in it, to be altogether with-it, brought its own disadvantages, not least among them the loss of perspective. (Must remember to supply the antecedents for all those *its* at a later date.)

Tolstoy had no problem with the antecedent for it. In "The Death of Ivan Ilych," *it* is death, impure and unsimple. "It alone was true," Tolstoy has Ivan Ilych reflect. "Face to face with *It*," Tolstoy later writes. "And nothing to be done with *It*. Only look and shudder." I recently reread Tolstoy's terrifying story, and not the least terrifying thing about it, to someone who is about to turn fifty, is that poor Ivan Ilych, in the story, is only forty-five. And "the thought had suddenly come into his head: 'What if in reality my whole life has been wrong?'" Ivan Ilych's whole life, as Tolstoy leaves no doubt, has indeed been wrong, wasted on the inessential and the irrelevant, which is what makes his death so bitter. The power of Tolstoy's story is of course in making every reader above a certain age—forty, let us say—ask that same question of his own life: "What if in reality my whole life has been wrong?"

There really is no way around asking that question, though there are endless ways of providing elusive answers to it. I do not so much ask the question of myself directly as consider it indirectly through the yearning to change my life, or at least my world, which comes upon me periodically. A few years ago, for example, I felt a powerful urge to drop all intellectual work—to continue reading, to continue writing (though much less than I now do), but to take a job that would put me more in the stream of daily life. One day I confided this to a graduate student, who, I rather insensitively failed to consider, longed to do exactly the kind of work I was contemplating leaving. "My God," she said, "if you are not happy, I may just commit suicide." I tried to explain, but am fairly certain that I did not succeed. You live, an old saying has it, and you learn. You live, I myself find, and you yearn.

If you are anything like me, you yearn above all to go on living. Unlike Ponce de León, I have never searched for the fountain of youth, but I should be heartily pleased if I could find a way to freeze time. Unlike, too, Mr. John McSorley, the founder of McSorley's Old Ale House (written about so splendidly by Joseph Mitchell), who, upon ceasing to drink at age fifty-five, was supposed to have announced, "I've had my share," I feel nothing of the kind about life. "If you're fifty-five and retired," runs the beginning of a commercial for an insurance company, and every time I hear it I think, "Wait a minute, I am fifty and have only begun." It's a fine age, fifty, an age when one begins to feel a certain ease in the world and mastery over one's environment, and I should like to remain at fifty for another twenty or thirty years. Somehow I have the sense that this will not be permitted.

At fifty one begins to be comfortable with oneself, but the more comfortable one feels, the more uncomfortably one feels time running out. The minutes, the hours, the days go as slowly as ever; it is those damn weeks, months, and years that now speed past. While I remain as youthful and beautiful as always, why, I cannot help ask, have so many of my contemporaries grown to look so old? It feels as if I have just arrived at the table, and they are already bringing out dessert; I have just stepped out onto the dance floor, and the band is getting ready to play "The Party's Over." Hold the waiters! Stop the music! I like it here. I don't want to leave.

And yet am I ready to do everything possible to stay? It is not always easy to distinguish between the love of life and the fear of death. ("It" again.) Nor are love of life and greed for it quite the same thing. I have acquaintances who—out of a love of life? a fear of death?—are slowly but rather systematically eliminating life's little physical pleasures: cutting out tobacco, alcohol, caffeine, red meat, cholesterol-laden food, all sugar. Soon their meals will be reduced to three dandelions and a nice cup of boiled water. These same people also generally torture themselves with exercise. (I like very much the saying that jogging extends one's life—but only by exactly the amount of time that one spends jogging.) Why do I find all this mildly upsetting, if not slightly obscene? It strikes me as greed for life, as opposed to love of life; it is a demonstration of people whose greed makes them willing to do anything for duration; and greed, even for good things, is not very pretty.

When I think of the distinction between the love of life and the greed for duration, I think of the writer A. J. Liebling. With the aid of his fork, Liebling had early joined the ranks of the obese, an army he was never to leave. Like many of the Frenchmen he knew of the generation before World War I—"the heroic age" of dining, he called it—Liebling never developed "the ulcers that come from worrying about a balanced diet." He did what he wanted to do; went where he wanted to go; wrote extremely well on those subjects he wished to write about; and lived with the throttle full-out—though a more appropriate metaphor would be "the plate always heaped up." Doubtless he would have lived longer had he lived more carefully. But had he lived more carefully—eaten less, drunk less—he would not have been A. J. Liebling. He had his fill and enjoyed the show, paying the check and leaving the table in his fifty-eighth year. Between the dandelion-and-boiled-water set and A. J. Liebling, a compromise position is possible. My own preference would be to live like Liebling and last until age ninety-seven. There is a contradiction here, I realize, but then, fortunately, the law of contradiction is not enforced, lest the jails overflow.

I can't supply a drumroll to go with this cliché, but the fact is that we human beings are the only species born with the painful foreknowledge of our death. Should this foreknowledge slip our minds, age is there as a perpetual crib, or pony, to remind us that life itself is a terminal illness. That at any rate is one way of looking at it. Another is to disregard age, as did Johnny Nikanov, a.k.a. King Cockeye Johnny, the gypsy who also appears in Joseph Mitchell's *McSorley's Wonderful Saloon* and who, when asked about his age, answered, "Between forty-five and seventy-five, somewhere in there. My hair's been white for years and years, and I got seventeen grandchildren, and I bet I'm an old, old man." There is something immensely appealing about that—about, more specifically, living outside age.

Most of us, I suspect, live our lives between these two possibilities, recalling that life is a terminal illness while at the same time forgetting our age. Our age seems incidental, something that has happened to us that we hadn't a great deal to do with, or that happened while we weren't looking. Sometimes our age frankly astonishes us; it is as if it were a strange country we suddenly find ourselves in. Fifty, one says. How the devil did I get here? If one thinks of age as a phonograph record, for many people the needle of their spirit seems to have stuck well before their actual age. I know a woman in her eighties who carries herself as if she were, tops, thirty-four. Despite the depredations of time and the ravages of illness, she is still, somehow, in spirit, sexy. I knew a man in his seventies in whom the mischievous eyes of a boy of eleven shone. My problem, if problem it be, is that I am and feel and look—fifty.

As ages go, and as long as one has to have some age, I am rather fond of fifty. It has a nice middling sound to it. It qualifies for the French phrase *d'un certain âge,* which I render, idiomatically, as "not so young." Yet neither is it all that old. It is roughly two-thirds up the mountain, not a bad place to view those thirty years below as well as those thirty or more years above. Fifty is an age old enough for one to have suffered serious disappointments, yet young enough not to be completely out of hope. Proust, who died at age fifty-one, wished to recapture time, and came as close in his great novel as anyone is likely to get; I, at fifty, will settle for allowing time to continue to run. "Miles to go before I sleep," the poet wrote, and I hope his words apply to me. Even now I am planning on being a colorful elderly dude, filled with rich and dubious stories. Should I achieve eighty years, I just may claim to have played ball with Jackie Robinson, to have danced for Diaghilev, to have been Anton Chekhov's gin-rummy partner. At that time, feel free to call me a liar, an outrageous old codger, even gaga. But call me a senior citizen and you had better carry dental insurance.

Reasons of the Body

SCOTT RUSSELL SANDERS

SCOTT RUSSELL SANDERS a professor of English at the University of Indiana, has written science fiction, literary criticism, short stories, and folklore, but recently has concentrated on the personal essay. His books of essays include *The Paradise of Bombs* (1987), *Secrets of the Universe* (1992), and *Staying Put* (1993).

My son has never met a sport he did not like. I have met a few that left an ugly tingle—boxing and rodeo and pistol shooting, among others—but, then, I have been meeting them for forty-four years, Jesse only for twelve. Our ages are relevant to the discussion, because, on the hill of the sporting life, Jesse is midway up the slope and climbing rapidly, while I am over the crest and digging in my heels as I slip down.

"You still get around pretty well for an old guy," he told me last night after we had played catch in the park.

The catch we play has changed subtly in recent months, a change that dramatizes a shift in the forces binding father and son. Early on, when I was a decade younger and Jesse a toddler, I was the agile one, leaping to snare his wild throws. The ball we tossed in those days was rubbery and light, a bubble of air as big around as a soup bowl, easy for small hands to grab. By the time he started school, we were using a tennis ball, then we graduated to a softball, then to gloves and a baseball. His repertoire of catches and throws increased along with his vocabulary.

Over the years, as Jesse put on inches and pounds and grace, I still had to be careful how far and hard I threw, to avoid bruising his ribs or his pride. But this spring, when we began limbering up our arms, his throws came whistling at me with a zing that hurt my hand, and he caught effortlessly anything I could hurl back at him. It was as though the food he wolfed down all winter had turned into spring steel. I no longer needed to hold back. Now Jesse is the one, when he is feeling charitable, who pulls his pitches.

Yesterday in the park, he was feeling frisky rather than charitable. We looped the ball lazily back and forth awhile. Then he started backing away, backing away, until my shoulder twinged from the length of throws. Unsatisfied, he yelled, "Make me run for it!" So I flung the ball high and deep, low and wide, driving him over the grass, yet he loped easily wherever it flew, gathered it in, then whipped it back to me with stinging speed.

"Come on," he yelled, "put it where I can't reach it." I tried, ignoring the ache in my arm, and still he ran under the ball. He might have been gliding on a cushion of air, he moved so lightly. I was feeling heavy, and felt heavier by the minute as his return throws, grown suddenly and unaccountably wild, forced me to hustle back and forth, jump and dive.

"Hey," I yelled, waving my glove at him, "look where I'm standing!"

"Standing is right," he yelled back. "Let's see those legs move!" His next throw sailed over my head, and the ones after that sailed farther still, now left now right, out of my range, until I gave up even trying for them, and the ball thudded accusingly to the ground. By the time we quit, I was sucking air, my knees were stiffening, and my arm was ablaze with pain. Jesse trotted up, his T-shirt dry, his breathing casual. This was the moment he chose to clap me on the back and say, "You still get around pretty well for an old guy."

It was a line I might have delivered, as a cocky teenager, to my own father. In his sober hours and years, which are the hours and years I measure him by, he would have laughed and then challenged me to a round of golf or a bout of arm wrestling, contests he could still easily have won.

Whatever else these games may be, they are always contests. For many a boy, some playing field, some court or gym is the first arena in which he can outstrip his old man. For me, the arena was a concrete driveway, where I played basketball against my father, shooting at a rusty hoop that was mounted over the garage. He had taught me how to dribble, how to time my jump, how to follow through on my shots. To begin with, I could barely heave the ball to the basket, and he would applaud if I so much as banged the rim. I banged away, year by year, my bones lengthening, muscles thickening. I shuffled over the concrete to the jazz of bird song and the opera of thunderstorms. I practiced fervently, as though my life depended on putting the ball through the hoop, practiced when the driveway was dusted with pollen and when it was drifted with snow. From first light to twilight, while the chimney swifts spiraled out to feed on mosquitoes and the mosquitoes fed on me, I kept shooting, hour after hour. Many of those hours, Father was tinkering in the garage, which reverberated with the slap of my feet and the slam of the ball. There came a day when I realized that I could outleap him, outhustle and outshoot him. I began to notice his terrible breathing, terrible because I had not realized he could run short of air. I had not realized he could run short of anything. When he bent over and grabbed his knees, huffing, "You're too much for me," I felt at once triumphant and dismayed.

I still have to hold back when playing basketball with Jesse. But the day will come, and soon, when he grows taller and stronger, and he will be the one to show mercy. The only dessert I will be able to eat, if I am to avoid growing fat, will be humble pie. Even now my shots appear old-fashioned to him, as my father's arching two-handed heaves seemed antique to me. "Show me some of those Neanderthal moves," Jesse cries as we shoot around at a basket in the park. "Show me how they did it in the Stone Age!" I do show him, clowning and hot-dogging, wishing by turns to amuse and impress him. As I fake and spin, I am simultaneously father and son playing games forward and backward in time.

The game of catch, like other sports where body faces body, is a dialogue carried on with muscle and bone. One body speaks by throwing a ball or a punch, by lunging with a foil, smashing a backhand, kicking a shot toward the corner of the net; the other replies by swinging, leaping, dodging, tackling, parrying, balancing. As in lovemaking, this exchange may be a struggle for power or a sharing of pleasure. The call and response may be in the spirit of antiphonal singing, a making of music that neither person could have achieved alone, or it may be in the spirit of insults bellowed across a table.

When a father and son play sports, especially a game the son has learned from the father, every motive from bitter rivalry to mutual delight may enter in. At first eagerly, and then grudgingly, and at last unconsciously, the son watches how his father grips the ball, handles the glove, swings the bat. In just the same way, the son has watched how the father swings a hammer, how the father walks, jokes, digs, starts a car, gentles a horse, pays a bill, shakes hands, shaves. There is a season in one's growing up, beginning at about the age Jesse is now, when a son comes to feel his old man's example as a smothering weight. You must shrug free of it, or die. And so, if your father carries himself soldier straight, you begin to slouch; if he strides along with a swagger, you slink; if he talks in joshing Mississippi accents to anybody with ears, you shun strangers and swallow your drawl. With luck and time, you may come to accept that you bear in your own voice overtones of your father's. You may come to rejoice that your own least motion—kissing a baby or opening a jar—is informed by memories of how your father would have done it. Between the early delight and the late reconciliation, however, you must pass through that season of rivalry, the son striving to undo or outdo his father's example, the father chewing on the bitter rind of rejection.

Why do I speak only of boys and men? Because, while there are females aplenty who relish any sport you can name, I have never shared a roof with one. In her seventies, my mother still dances and swims, even leads classes in aerobics, but she's never had much use for games played with balls, and neither has my wife or daughter. When Ruth, my wife, was a child, a bout of rheumatic fever confined her to bed and then to a wheelchair for several years. Until she was old enough for university, a heart rendered tricky by the illness kept her from doing anything that would raise her pulse, and by then she had invested her energies elsewhere, in music and science. To this day, Ruth sees no point in moving faster than a walk, or in defying gravity with exuberant leaps, or in puzzling over the trajectory of a ball.

And what of our daughter, sprightly Eva, firstborn? Surely I could have brought her up to become a partner for catch? Let me assure you that I tried. I put a sponge ball in her crib, as Father had put a baseball in mine. (I was going to follow tradition exactly and teethe her on a baseball, but Ruth, sensible of a baby's delicacy, said nothing doing.) From the moment the nurse handed Eva to me in the hospital, a quivering bundle, ours to keep, I coached my spunky girl, I coaxed and exhorted her, but she would not be persuaded that throwing or kicking a ball was a sensible way to spend an hour or an afternoon. After seventeen years of all the encouragement that love can buy, the one sport she will deign to play with me is volleyball, in which she hurtles over the grass, leaping and cavorting, as only a dancer could.

As a dancer and gymnast, Eva has always been on good terms with her body, and yet, along with her mother and my mother, she rolls her eyes when Jesse and I begin rummaging in the battered box on the porch for a baseball, basketball, or soccer ball. "So Dad," she calls, "it's off to recover past glories, is it? You show 'em, tiger. But don't break any bones."

Eva's amusement has made the opinion of the women in my life unanimous. Their baffled indulgence, bordering at times on mockery, has given to sports a tang of the mildly illicit.

Like many other women (not all, not all), those in my family take even less interest in talking about sports than in playing them. They pride themselves on being above such idle gab. They shake their heads when my son and I check the scores in the newspaper. They are astounded that we can spend longer rehashing a game than we spent in playing it. When Jesse and I compare aches after a session on field or court, the women observe mildly that it sounds as though we had been mugged. Surely we would not inflict such damage on ourselves? Perhaps we have gotten banged up from wrestling bears? We kid along and say, "Yes, we ran into the Chicago Bears," and my daughter or mother or wife will reply, "You mean the hockey team?"

In many households and offices, gossip about games and athletes breaks down along gender lines, the men indulging in it and the women scoffing. Those on each side of the line may exaggerate their feelings, the men pumping up their enthusiasm, the women their indifference, until sport becomes a male mystery. No locker room, no sweat lodge is needed to shut women out; mere talk will do it. Men are capable of muttering about wins and losses, batting averages and slam dunks, until the flowers on the wallpaper begin to wilt and every woman in the vicinity begins to yearn for a supply of gags. A woman friend of mine, an executive in a computing firm, has been driven in self-defense to scan the headlines of the sports pages before going to work, so that she can toss out references to the day's contests and stars, like chunks of meat, to feed the appetites of her male colleagues. After gnawing on this bait, the men may consent to speak with her of things more in keeping with her taste, such as books, birds, and the human condition.

My daughter has never allowed me to buy her a single item of sports paraphernalia. My son, on the other hand, has never said no to such an offer. Day and night, visions of athletic gear dance in his head. With religious zeal, he pores over magazine ads for sneakers, examining the stripes and insignia as if they were hieroglyphs of ultimate truth. Between us, Jesse and I are responsible for the hoard of equipment on our back porch, which contains at present the following items: one bicycle helmet and two bicycles; a volleyball set, badminton set, and a bag of golf clubs; three racquets for tennis, two for squash, one for paddleball; roller skates and ice skates, together with a pair of hockey sticks; goalie gloves, batting gloves, three baseball gloves and one catcher's mitt; numerous yo-yos; ten pairs of cleated or waffle-soled shoes; a drying rack festooned with shorts and socks and shirts and sweatsuits; and a cardboard box heaped with (I counted) forty-nine balls, including ones for all the sports implicated above, as well as for Ping-Pong, lacrosse, juggling, and jacks.

Excavated by some future archaeologist, this porch full of gear would tell as much about how we passed our lives as would the shells and seeds and bones of a kitchen midden. An excavation of the word *sport* also yields evidence of breaks, bruises, and ambiguities. A sport is a game, all orderly zone marked off from the prevailing disorder, but it can also he a mutation, a violation of rules. To be good at sports is to be a winner, and yet a good sport is one who loses amiably, a bad sport one who kicks and screams at every setback. A flashy dresser might be called a sport, and so might a gambler, an idler, an easygoing companion, one who dines high on the hog of pleasure. But the same label may be attached to one who is the butt of jokes, a laughingstock, a goat. As a verb, to sport can mean to wear jewelry or clothes in a showy manner, to poke fun, to trifle, to roll promiscuously in the hay. It is a word spiced with unsavory meanings, rather tacky and cheap, with hints of brothels, speakeasies, and malodorous dives. And yet it bears also the wholesome flavor of fairness, vigor, and ease.

The lore of sports may be all that some fathers have to pass down to their sons in place of lore about hunting animals, planting seeds, killing enemies, or placating the gods. Instead of telling him how to shoot a buffalo, the father whispers in the son's ear how to shoot a lay-up. Instead of consulting the stars or the entrails of birds, father and son consult the smudged print of newspapers to see how their chosen spirits are faring. They fiddle with the dials of radios, hoping to catch the oracular murmur of a distant game. The father recounts heroic deeds, not from the field of battle, but from the field of play. The seasons about which he speaks lead not to harvests but to championships. No longer intimate with the wilderness, no longer familiar even with the tamed land of farms, we create artificial landscapes bounded by lines of paint or lime. Within those boundaries, as within the frame of a chessboard or painting, life achieves a memorable, seductive clarity. The lore of sports is a step down from that of nature, perhaps even a tragic step, but it is lore nonetheless, with its own demigods and demons, magic and myths.

The sporting legends I carry from my father are private rather than public. I am haunted by scenes that no journalist recorded, no camera filmed. Father is playing a solo round of golf, for example, early one morning in April. The fairways glisten with dew. Crows rasp and fluster in the pines that border the course. Father lofts a shot toward a par-3 hole, and the white ball arcs over the pond, over the sand trap, over the shaggy apron of grass onto the green, where it bounces, settles down then rolls toward the flag, rolls unerringly, inevitably, until it falls with a scarcely audible click into the hole. The only eyes within sight besides his own are the crows'. For once, the ball has obeyed him perfectly, harmonizing wind and gravity and the revolution of the spheres, one shot has gone where all are meant to go, and there is nobody else to watch. He stands on the tee, gazing at the distant hole, knowing what he has done and that he will never do it again. The privacy of this moment appeals to me more than all the clamor and fame of a shot heard round the world.

Here is another story I live by: the man who will become my father is twenty-two, a catcher for a bush-league baseball team in Tennessee. He will never make it to the majors, but on weekends he earns a few dollars for squatting behind the plate and nailing runners foolish enough to try stealing second base. From all those bus rides, all those red-dirt diamonds, the event he will describe for his son with deepest emotion is an exhibition game. Father's team of whites, most of them fresh from two-mule farms, is playing a touring black team, a rare event for that day and place. To make it even rarer, and the sides fairer, the coaches agree to mix the teams. And so my father, son of a Mississippi cotton farmer, bruised with racial notions that will take a lifetime to heal, crouches behind the plate and for nine innings catches fastballs and curves, change-ups and screwballs from a whirling, muttering wizard of the Negro Baseball League, one Leroy Robert Paige, known to the world as Satchel. Afterward, Satchel Paige tells the farm boy, "You catch a good game," and the farm boy answers, "You've got the stuff, mister." And for the rest of my father's life, this man's pitching serves as a measure of mastery.

And here is a third myth I carry: One evening when the boy who will become my father is eighteen, he walks into the Black Cat Saloon in Tupelo, Mississippi. He is looking for a fight. Weary of plowing, sick of red dirt, baffled by his own turbulent energy, he often picks fights. This evening the man he picks on is a stranger who occupies a nearby stool at the bar, a husky man in his thirties, wearing a snap-brim hat, dark suit with wide lapels, narrow tie, and an infuriatingly white shirt. The stranger is slow to anger. The red-headed Sanders boy keeps at him, keeps at him, mocking the Yankee accent, the hat worn indoors, the monkey suit, the starched shirt, until at last the man stands up and backs away from the bar, fists raised. The Sanders boy lands three punches, he remembers that much, but the next thing he remembers is waking up on the sidewalk, the stranger bending over him to ask if he is all right, and to ask, besides, if he would like a boxing scholarship to Mississippi State. The man is headed there to become the new coach. The boy who will become my father goes to Mississippi State for two years, loses some bouts and wins more, then quits to pursue a Golden Gloves title. When he fails at that, he keeps on fighting in bars and streets, until at last he quits boxing, his nose broken so many times there is no bone left in it, only a bulb of flesh which a boy sitting in his lap will later squeeze and mash like dough. From all those bouts, the one he will describe to his son with the greatest passion is that brawl from the Black Cat Saloon, when the stranger in the shirt, a good judge of fighters, found him worthy.

Father tried, with scant success, to make a boxer of me. Not for a career in the ring, he explained, but for defense against the roughs and rowdies who would cross my path in life. If I ran into a mean customer, I told him, I could always get off the path. No, Father said, a man never backs away. A man stands his ground and fights. This advice ran against my grain, which inclined toward quickness of wits rather than fists, yet for years I strove to become the tough guy he envisioned. Without looking for fights, I stumbled into them at every turn, in schoolyard and backyard and in the shadows of barns. Even at my most belligerent, I still tried cajolery and oratory first. Only when that failed did I dig in my heels and start swinging. I gave bruises and received them, gave and received bloody noses, leading with my left, as Father had taught me, protecting my head with forearms, keeping my thumbs outside my balled fists to avoid breaking them when I landed a punch.

Some bullies saw my feistiness as a red flag. One boy who kept hounding me was Olaf Magnuson, a neighbor whose surname I would later translate with my primitive Latin as Son of Big. The name was appropriate, for Olaf was two years older and a foot taller and forty pounds heavier than I was. He pestered me, cursed me, irked and insulted me. When I stood my ground, he pounded me into it. One evening in my twelfth summer, after I had staggered home several times from these frays bloodied and bowed, Father decided it was time for serious boxing lessons. We would train for two months, he told me, then challenge Olaf Magnuson to a fight, complete with gloves and ropes and bell. This did not sound like a healthy idea to me; but Father insisted. "Do you want to keep getting pushed around," he demanded, "or are you going to lick the tar out of him?"

Every day for two months I ran, skipped rope, did chin-ups and push-ups. Father hung his old punching bag from a rafter in the basement, and I flailed at it until my arms filled with sand. He wrapped an old mattress around a tree and told me to imagine Olaf Magnuson's belly as I pounded the cotton ticking. I sparred with my grizzly old man, who showed me how to jab and hook, duck and weave, how to keep my balance and work out of corners. Even though his feet had slowed, his hands were still so quick that I sometimes dropped my own gloves to watch him, dazzled. "Keep Up those dukes," he warned. "Never lower your guard." For two months I trained as though I had a boxer's heart.

Father issued our challenge by way of Olaf Magnuson's father, a strapping man with a voice like a roar in a barrel. Hell yes, my boy'll fight, the elder Magnuson boomed.

On the morning appointed for our bout, Father strung rope from tree to tree in the yard, fashioning a ring that was shaped like a lozenge. My mother, who had been kept in the dark about the grudge match until that morning, raised sand for a while; failing to make us see what fools we were, disgusted with the ways of men, she drove off to buy groceries. My sister carried word through the neighborhood and within minutes a gaggle of kids and a scattering of bemused adults pressed against the ropes.

"You're going to make that lunkhead bawl in front of the whole world," Father told me in the kitchen while lacing my gloves. "You're going to make him call for his mama. Before you're done with him, he's going to swallow so many teeth that he'll never mess with you again."

So long as Father was talking, I believed him. I was a mean hombre. I was bad news, one fist of iron and the other one steel. When he finished his pep talk, however, and we stepped out into the sunshine, and I saw the crowd buzzing against the ropes, and I spied enormous Olaf slouching from his own kitchen door, my confidence hissed away like water on a hot griddle. In the seconds it took me to reach the ring, I ceased to feel like the bringer of bad news and began to feel like the imminent victim. I danced in my corner, eyeing Olaf. His torso, hulking above jeans and clodhopper boots, made my own scrawny frame look like a preliminary sketch for a body. I glanced down at my ropy arms, at my twiggy legs exposed below red gym shorts, at my high-topped basketball shoes, at the grass.

"He'll be slow," Father growled in my ear, "slow and clumsy. Keep moving. Bob and weave. Give him the left jab, watch for an opening, and then *bam*, unload with the right."

Not trusting my voice, I nodded, and kept shuffling my sneakers to hide the shivers.

Father put his palms to my cheeks and drew my face close to his and looked hard at me. Above that smushed, boneless nose, his brown eyes were as dark and shiny as those of a deer. "You okay, big guy?" he asked. "You ready for this?" I nodded again. "Then go get him," he said, turning me around and giving me a light shove toward the center of the ring.

I met Olaf there for instructions from the referee, a welder who lived down the road from us, a wiry man with scorched forearms who had just fixed our trailer hitch. I lifted my eyes reluctantly from Olaf's boots, along the trunks of his jean-clad legs, over the expanse of brawny chest and palooka jaw to his ice blue eyes. They seemed less angry than amused.

A cowbell clattered. Olaf and I touched gloves, backed apart and lifted our mitts. The crowd sizzled against the ropes. Blood banged in my ears, yet I could hear Father yelling. I hear him still. And in memory I follow his advice. I bob, I weave, I guard my face with curled gloves, I feint and jab within the roped diamond. I begin to believe in myself; I circle my lummoxy rival, and pepper him with punches; I feel a grin rising to my lips, and then Olaf tires of the game and rears back and knocks me flat. He also knocks me out. He also breaks my nose, which will remain crooked forever after.

That ended my boxing career. Olaf quit bullying me, perhaps because my blackout had given him a scare, perhaps because he had proved whatever he needed to prove. What I had shown my father was less clear. He may have seen weakness, may have seen a doomed and reckless bravery, may have seen a clown's pratfall. In any case, he never again urged me to clear the path with my fists.

And I have not offered boxing lessons to my son. Instead, I offered him the story of my defeat. When Jesse would still fit in my lap, I cuddled him there and told of my fight with Olaf, and he ran his delicate finger against the crook in my nose, as I had fingered the boneless pulp

of Father's nose. I told Jesse about learning to play catch, the ball passing back and forth like a thread between my father and me, stitching
us together. I told him about the time one of my pitches sailed over
Father's head and shattered the windshield of our 1956 Ford, a car
just three days old, and Father only shook his head and said, "Shoot,
boy, you get that fastball down, and the batters won't see a thing but
smoke." And I told Jesse about sitting on a feather tick in a Mississippi
farmhouse, wedged between my father and grandfather, shaking with
their excitement while before us on a tiny black-and-white television
two boxers slammed and hugged each other. Cradling my boy, I felt
how difficult it is for men to embrace without the liquor of violence,
the tonic of pain.

Why do we play these games so avidly? All sports, viewed dispas-
sionately, are dumb. The rules are arbitrary, the behaviors absurd.
For boxing and running, perhaps, you could figure out evolutionary
advantages. But what earthly use is it to become expert at swatting a
ball with a length of wood or at lugging an inflated pigskin through
a mob? Freudians might say that in playing with balls we men are
simply toying with the prize portion of our anatomies. Darwinians
might claim that we are competing for the attention of females, like so
many preening peacocks or head-butting rams. Physicians might at-
tribute the sporting frenzy to testosterone; economists might point to
our dreams of professional paychecks; feminists might appeal to our
machismo; philosophers, to our fear of death.

No doubt all of those explanations, like buckets put out in the rain,
catch some of the truth. But none of them catches all of the truth.
None of them explains, for example, what moves a boy to bang a
rubber ball against a wall for hours, for entire summers, as my father
did in his youth, as I did in mine, as Jesse still does. That boy, throwing
and catching in the lee of garage or barn, dwells for a time wholly in

his body, and that is reward enough. He aims the ball at a knothole, at a crack, then leaps to snag the rebound, mastering a skill, working himself into a trance. How different is his rapture from the dancing and drumming of a young brave? How different is his solitude from that of any boy seeking visions?

The less use we have for our bodies, the more we need reminding that the body possesses its own way of knowing. To steal a line from Pascal: The body has its reasons that reason knows nothing of. Although we struggle lifelong to dwell in the flesh without rancor, without division between act and desire, we succeed only for moments at a time. We treasure whatever brings us those moments, whether it be playing cello or playing pool, making love or making baskets, kneading bread, or nursing a baby or kicking a ball. Whoever teaches us an art or skill, whoever shows us a path to momentary wholeness, deserves our love.

I am conscious of my father's example whenever I teach a game to my son. Demonstrating a move in basketball, I amplify my gestures, like a ham actor playing to the balcony. My pleasure in the part is increased by the knowledge that others, and especially Father, have played it before me. What I know about hitting a curve or shooting a hook shot or throwing a left jab, I know less by words than by feel. When I take Jesse's hand and curl his fingers over the baseball's red stitches, explaining how to make it deviously spin, I feel my father's hands slip over mine like gloves. Move like so, like so. I feel the same ghostly guidance when I hammer nails or fix a faucet or pluck a banjo. Working on the house or garden or car, I find myself wearing more than my father's hands, find myself clad entirely in his skin.

One blistering afternoon when I was a year younger than Jesse is now, a fly ball arched toward me in center field. I ran under it, lifted my face and glove, and lost the ball in the sun. The ball found me, however, crashing into my eye. In the split second before blacking out

I saw nothing but light. We need not go hunting pain, for pain will find us. It hurts me more to see Jesse ache than to break one of my own bones. I cry out as the ground ball bangs into his throat. I wince as he comes down crookedly with a rebound and turns his ankle. I wish to spare him injury as I wish to spare him defeat, but I could not do so even if I had never lobbed him that first fat pitch.

As Jesse nears thirteen, his estimate of my knowledge and my power declines rapidly. He sees me slipping down the far slope. If I were a potter, say, or a carpenter, my skills would outreach his for decades to come. But where speed and stamina are the essence, a father in his forties will be overtaken by a son in his teens. Training for soccer, Jesse carries a stopwatch as he jogs around the park. I am not training for anything, only knocking rust from my joints and beguiling my heart, but I run along with him, puffing to keep up. I know that his times will keep going down, while I will never run faster than I do now. This is as it should be, for his turn has come. Slow as I am, and doomed to be slower, I relish his company.

In the game of catch, this dialogue of throw and grab we have been carrying on since he was old enough to crawl, Jesse has finally begun to put questions that I cannot answer. I know the answers; I can see how my back should twist, my legs should pump; but legs and back will no longer match my vision. This faltering is the condition of our lives, of course, a condition that will grow more acute with each passing year. I mean to live the present year before rushing off to any future ones. I mean to keep playing games with my son, so long as flesh will permit, as my father played games with me well past his own physical prime. Now that sports have begun to give me lessons in mortality, I realize they have also been giving me, all the while, lessons in immortality. These games, these contests, these grunting conversations of body to body, father to son, are not substitutes for some other way of being alive. They are the sweet and sweaty thing itself.

The Wind Did It

BERNARD COOPER

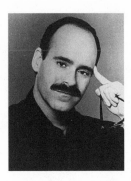

BERNARD COOPER teaches writing at the University of California at Los Angeles. He was born in Hollywood, California, and studied at the California Institute of the Arts. His first book of essays, *Maps to Anywhere* (1992), won the Associated Writing Program's award for creative nonfiction.

Sleeping with My Father

My father glances at an airplane in the distance and tells me this story as he drives down the street:

"Remember when Mrs. King lived next door? Well, she used to work as a chaperone for *The Dating Game* and one day a couple won a trip to Israel and she went with them. TWA I think it was. And she told me that toward the end of the flight a stewardess comes over to where the three of them are sitting and asks would they move back a few rows. So they do, kind of confused, and then these Israelis in uniform come out of the cockpit, dismantle some seats, set up machine guns and aim them out the windows. Mrs. King—remember how nice she was?—anyway, she got very upset. Who wouldn't? And she says to the stewardess, she says, 'Dear, level with me. What's with the ammo?' and the stewardess says, 'Just a precautionary measure. Terrorists. You know. . . . We've never had cause to fire.'"

"Dad," I ask, "did you believe her?"

"Tell me, Mr. Skeptic," he says, lifting both hands from the steering wheel in order to shrug his shoulders, "why would a stewardess lie?"

"No," I moan. "Did you believe Mrs. King?"

My father blinks, remains silent. He adjusts his glasses, the broken stem held together by a clot of electrical tape. His white hair gleams with Brylcreem.

"Look, Pop," I say, "if the windows of the airplane were open, all the passengers, Mrs. King included, would be sucked into the stratosphere. Poof. Gone."

"Yeah, yeah. Maybe you have a point. It's a good story, though." He flicks a switch marked AIR, and in seconds the inside of the car is arctic. "I don't know why I brought it up," he says. "I was just thinking. I was just looking back."

For nearly a year, my father has been divorced from his second wife, Esther, a black elementary-school teacher and devout Catholic forty years his junior. She has yet to retrieve her possessions from his house, the Spanish house in which I grew up, its walls and vestibules still crowded with their combined religious artifacts: his statuette of Moses in windblown robes, hoisting the Ten Commandments; her oil painting of Jesus gazing heavenward, pious, pale. Crosses and Stars of David vie for attention in every room. These, combined with heavy Mediterranean furniture, give his house an inquisitional air.

During his three-year marriage to Esther, my father and I rarely saw each other. In an attempt to "turn over a new leaf," as he so often put it, he summarily jettisoned from his life those people and things that bound him to the past: my mother's jewelry—she'd made no provision for it in her will—was pawned; the house was repainted a pale chartreuse with chocolate trim (Mrs. King would have been appalled); and as for me, his thirty-five-year-old baby, I was, so to speak, tossed out with the bath water. Once, though, I ran into him at the supermarket, his "new leaf" manifest in a little dance I saw him do down the aisle: he swayed in rhythm behind the cart as he grabbed at cinnamon coffee cake, tubes of juice, bags of Esther's favorite candy, Muzak humming into the air from some lofty, mysterious source—the ceiling, the spheres; it didn't matter. Dad was entranced in a dance of veils, burdens flung from his aging body.

These idyllic days were numbered, however. Unlike my father, Esther brought with her to the marriage the full force of her past, a hidden past which included bouts of depression, a melancholy undiminished by regimens of exercise or psychotropic drugs. She spent weeks languishing in bed, mute and inconsolable, her jaw clenched, the shades drawn. Just how my father dealt with Esther's descent into despair—and finally rage—I'm not certain, but I know my father well enough to speculate that he must have tickled her, crooned songs, made faces, regaled her with gifts, utterly mystified as to why his kindness and cajoling had no effect. His new wife was deaf to his entreaties, her tempting figure was wrapped in blankets, her eyes extinguished. He interpreted Esther's condition as an affront, proof that his reserves of playfulness, his romantic machinations would come to nothing, proof that, in the end, the troubled life he tried to escape could not be pawned or painted away.

His past washed back, and I rode with it.

More and more these days I keep him company. He'll drive us to Art's Prime Rib, his favorite restaurant, and always we seem to head toward the sun. The visors are no help; a glare, intense and tropical, saturates his Cadillac, and there, at the end of the street, the summer sun consumes the horizon, branding hotspots on the Caddy's hood.

I've never told him that I read the article about his divorce suit in the *Herald Examiner*. His claims against Esther must have struck the reporter as sufficiently preposterous to warrant space under Local News. The headline read, "One for the Three Bears: Suit Filed in Bed Rights Fight." The copy spared no details:

Attorney Edward S. Cooper's wife didn't take kindly to his decision
to retire for the night in her bedroom, according to a $25,000 law-
suit Cooper filed against Mrs. Cooper yesterday. In fact, Cooper
said, his wife, Esther Williams Cooper, brandished a 12-inch knife,
punched him repeatedly and smashed his eyeglasses while demanding that he get out. As a result, Cooper's suit contends, the
attorney suffered "severe shock ... severe pain in the right ear ... is
in fear of becoming totally deaf, thereby losing his right to earn his
livelihood from his profession." He also suffered a groin injury and
a cut under his left eye.

According to the Superior Court action, the assault took place
on July 9, when Mrs. Cooper found her eighty-year-old husband
sleeping in her bedroom of their Hollywood home. The Coopers
had occupied separate bedrooms since May 30, the suit said.

I offer the above excerpt not as evidence of the humiliation my father no doubt endured when this article appeared, nor as a way of sub-
stantiating events that otherwise seem exaggerated for literary effect;
rather, I offer it so that one might better understand how, as my father
and I drive to dinner, my secret knowledge of him, acquired via the
news, hangs between us like a crystal chandelier, swaying and clinking,
erupting with refractions.

My father's history can be divided into three distinct phases. During
my boyhood and his marriage to my mother until her death, my father
was a man wracked by an excess of energy. He never seemed to sleep.
His was not the insomnia that results in indolence, bags beneath the
eyes, stifled yawns. When he was awake he was *wide* awake, jumping at
the slightest noise. No exertion, regardless how back-breaking, could
exhaust him completely. On Sundays, he gardened our yard till sun-
set, unshaven and glazed with sweat. Nights were devoted to pacing,

a record of his aimless trails and quick pivots crushed into the carpet. He brought work home from his office by the armload, teetering stacks of depositions, dog-eared files. He even ate in nervous surges, spearing and gulping, his face flushed, the veins in his temples blue. Sometimes my mother and I would balk at his fervor, our own forkfuls frozen mid-air, and we'd stare at each other and then at my father who'd grumble "What," his mouth still full.

The next, or newlywed period, was, as I've mentioned, characterized by abandon, buoyancy, boyishness. The blood that had once banged through his head had somehow turned to helium. On my way home from work once, I saw my father's Cadillac parked in the lot of the local florists, and I pictured him offering blossoms to Esther, beaming above a prodigious bouquet. Apart from flowers and his dance to Muzak, let the following list of objects stand for this phase of my father's life: a cassette of Tony Bennett's greatest hits, a pair of Sergio Valenti jeans with gold piping, a cherrywood box in which were kept the corks he's coaxed from bottles of champagne.

The third and current phase began after he made the *Herald*. It is, to me, the most astonishing of all. Yes, he is lonely, remorseful, baffled at dawn in his infamous bed. Strangely though, he is never despondent, but talkative, gentle, tempered by troubles. Without warning or preamble, without so much as clearing his throat, he'll launch into some story, the gist of which is comparison, comparison for its own sweet sake:

"See that dog food billboard? Well, once my brother and I had a dog. A schnauzer. Brown. Sammy or something . . ."

"And . . . ?"

"That's it, boychik. I was just thinking. I was just looking back."

Driving to dinner with my father is like entering a chamber in which Then and Now collide and coalesce, the narrative equivalent of nuclear fusion. This dreamy world view of his is infectious, and I've caught myself more than once gazing out the car window, engaged in thoughts that vacillate between the present and the past, ending finally in pleasant limbo between the two. I've noticed that my father and I are starting to look and sound alike. Our voices share a Semitic inflection, each bit of banter rising slightly, every sentence becoming a question. Should we pass some lunatic flailing his arms and orating on the corner, we'll both expel a breath of air and slap our cheeks in disbelief. My hair is receding just as his did. We each have long lashes, clefts in our chins, a mole at the base of our throats. Maybe it's the blazing sun that accentuates the traits we share.

In those moments when we've nothing left to talk about, I imagine that my father and I, heat-baked, squinting, will ride together to the end of the earth, the car careening toward the center of the sun, our lives ignited in a sudden conflagration, our fates melded in a blast of light.

I had a dream about my father. I dreamed it after his divorce from Esther, after his loneliness became clear to me, after he'd begun to tell meandering stories, after we'd shared a few dinners together, after I'd begun to recognize the ways in which we're alike. I came to him in his bedroom. He was sleeping in the center of a double bed. The room was suffused with blue light. It was dusk or dawn, I didn't know. On the dresser, statuettes of Moses and Jesus oversaw our assignation. I stroked his shoulder. My father awoke. "Dad," I whispered, "are we getting older?" "Here," he said, lifting the blanket. "Here," he said, patting the bed.

Machu Picchu

Since his divorce from Esther, my father has read *Secrets of the Maya* five times. The paperback lies like a Bible on his nightstand. I've yet to ask him how his obsession with the Maya began, but my rare ventures into his bedroom during the past year have yielded a theory. Esther redecorated the room in a vivid collision of colors—orange afghan, purple lamp shades, wallpaper flocked with blue flowers—which no doubt intensify my father's insomnia. And this paperback book, with its tales of the ancients playing handball, inventing calendars, climbing the steps of pyramids, offers my father hours of escape from a room that vibrates with Esther's presence.

Still, it's only a theory, and tonight over dinner at Art's Prime Rib, I ask my father if he would try to articulate just what it is about this particular civilization that intrigues him. For a moment he appears not to hear me and continues to blow on a spoonful of soup. Then he looks up. Thick glasses magnify his eyes. He pushes his French onion soup aside, places his palms on the table.

"First of all," he says, "they worshiped everything there was to worship, like, um, corn. . . ." He drums his fingers, stumped. "You know—things . . . buildings. And they made contributions to the societies of today, like x-ray."

"X-ray?"

"Yeah. Well, not x-ray. But they carved stone pictures of people's insides. Pregnant women and where their babies would be, or just your average Mayas with lungs and livers. Now I'm not saying that these were actual x-rays as we know them, but you have to start somewhere, right? I mean, how'd they think of these things? Shirley McLaine, the actress, the one who wrote that book *Tree* something . . ."

"*Out on a Limb.*"

My father snaps his fingers. "Limb, that's it. Anyway, she thinks the Mayas and Aztecs and Incas were advanced people from another planet. I'm not saying I believe her, see, but it *is* food for thought. Boychik," he adds, plucking a radish from a bowl of ice, "the world is full of unanswered questions."

The waiter appears with our salads. He dangles a pepper mill over the table. My father waves it away.

Silence punctuated by the crunch of lettuce.

"Hey," he blurts. "How'd you like to visit Machu Picchu with me?"

"Machu Picchu?"

"Whadd'ya say we go there. Together." My father leans forward, his expression so sincere, his voice so plaintive, I think he might try to kiss me. "The Lost City," he says. His moist eyes catch the candlelight.

I can't answer my father immediately; I'm dizzy with mountain peaks, black and green, slicing huge and fluid clouds, the air so thin it muffles sound. Even parrots avoid this height. My father sits on a crumbling wall, holding his knees and breathing hard. "Oy," he heaves. "We're actually here. Give the donkeys something to drink."

The steam from a mound of mashed potatoes eases me out of my fantasy. As tempting as his offer sounds, as much as it appeals to my desire to be, for the first time, his loyal son, I've never taken a trip alone with my father, and to attempt one now might jeopardize the intimacy we've recently achieved.

"Nice that you asked, Dad. But I really can't afford it."

"Afford? I'll pay."

"I . . . my classes."

"Summer then."

"I teach in the summer, too."

"O.K.," he says. He turns up his hearing aid and flinches at its high-pitched whistle. "You can't say I didn't try."

"I ought to get rid of this place," my father says when we return from dinner. He fumbles for the key to the door. "It's too damn big for one person." Behind us in the driveway, the Cadillac ticks as the engine cools. "Ta-da," Dad sings when he finds the right key.

There are in my life a small number of sensations which never seem to vary or diminish: a sudden chill at the sight of blood, numbness in the legs induced by heights. To these may be added the sensation of entering my father's house, the odors layered and playing like music: a counterpoint of plastic and wood, a musty undertone coming from the rugs, my father's lemon aftershave resounding within the walls.

I follow my father as he moves through the rooms and flicks on the lights. "I need all this?" he asks, pointing with both arms around the large living room. We sit opposite each other on identical velvet couches. I shrug and investigate the objects crowded on the coffee table: a souvenir brochure from John F. Kennedy's inauguration, a book of paintings by Norman Rockwell, an album with photos of my father and Esther, suntanned, smiling. "Dad," I ask. "where were these pictures taken?"

"Mexico," he mutters. He stares over my head and out the bay window. Twilight bathes his upturned face, accentuates lines and shadows. "Honeymoon," he continues, without looking at me. "Mayas." My father remains mesmerized for what seems like minutes, his body perfectly still, eyes fixed on some distant point. Dust motes drift through the air between us. Finally his gaze meets mine. "I'm stuffed," he says, patting his stomach. "How 'bout TV?"

We lumber upstairs to his bedroom, where my father keeps a widescreen Zenith. He opens a window, settles into a recliner and fiddles with the remote control. I sit near his feet. On *Jeopardy,* Alex Trebek, the game show's host, is reminding the three contestants that they will be shown answers, and must phrase their response in the form of a question.

"Jeez this game is tough," my father says. "I hardly ever get one right." He has strapped an electric massager to his hand. It begins to buzz. He touches his vibrating hand to my head. I shiver and arch my back against his knees. My father rakes his fingers through my hair, presses my scalp until everything trembles—the people on the screen, the table and ottoman flanking the set, the flowers flocked on the wall. My glasses slowly slide down my nose. Colors are jolted from the edges of objects, the room blurred and otherworldly. I worry I may lose control, begin to whimper or weep with pleasure.

"What is euthanasia?" screams my father. "Who was Woodrow Wilson?" He traces concentric circles on my temples, squeezes the nape of my neck. My ears are hot, my shoulders succumb to gravity. "What is a microchip? Who are the Mormon Tabernacle Choir? What is penicillin?" From the corner of my eye, through the shaking window, I see the jostled tops of trees, the quivering peaks of the Hollywood hills, faint stars wobbling in the sky. My father continues to work down my spine, calling questions into the night.

Father as Fountain

"No," says my father, "it wasn't my appendix." He changes lanes without looking.

"Kidney stones?" I ask. "Gall bladder?"

"For the life of me," says my father, smacking his forehead, "I can't remember what they took out of me. Whatever the hell it was, Bernard, I've felt a lot better these past few months." The Caddy's electric windows whir down. My father's baggy Hawaiian shirt flutters in the breeze.

"Have you lost weight, Dad?"

My father tries to look at his torso. "Maybe a little," he says. "The food the maid cooks is pretty bad. She cleans up beautiful though. I've still got to lose more. Doctor's orders."

Burning at the center of our discourse like the sun is the one subject we never miss, the subject which dwarfs and outshines all the others:

the state of our health. We carefully monitor every ache and crimp and itch. We talk about our blocked sinuses, fallen arches, ingrown hairs.

"Look at this red thing on my wrist," my father says at a stoplight.

"Oh, that's just a cherry angioma."

"A what?"

"Like a mole. But red. It's nothing."

"How da you . . . ?"

"*Scribners Dictionary of Medical Terms.* I'll get you a copy."

"You don't think it's . . ."

"Everybody has them. Believe me. I looked it up."

My father checks once more to be sure. He holds his wrist close to his face as though he were sampling a dab of cologne.

Our mutual fascination with the body and the countless ailments that might besiege it was brought about, in part, by my mother's life-long obsession with nutrition. She bought every book that extolled the virtues of vitamins, herbal remedies, or novel diets—*Rice for Life, Food Groups and You, A Practical Guide to Cooking with Parsley.* She once read that chopping vegetables breaks down their cellular structure to such an extent that the minerals are virtually useless. For weeks after, my father and I were served on pink plates, whole carrots (tops included), plump zucchinis, and bell peppers. When she read that Jewish folk wisdom was confirmed by doctors who found that chicken broth did, in fact, help cure colds, she had the kosher butcher deliver a trio of plucked and pale fowl. For years, on the advice of nutritionist Adele Davis, she plied my father and me with gallons of milk for healthy marrow. My mother was inconsolable when she heard that Adele Davis had died from bone cancer. She didn't mourn the woman herself. Rather, my mother mourned the hope that somewhere among the pages of her books was hidden the secret of sustenance, the key to our longevity.

All my relatives, to varying degrees, were preoccupied with physical well-being. Even as a child, when my parents played bridge with Aunt Flo and Uncle Sid, I'd be curled on the living-room couch, surfacing from a mild sleep to hear them whisper the strange words I sensed meant something bad about the body—*ulcer, lumbago, cataract.* The mention of these afflictions was followed by Father clicking his tongue.

"You've got to live for today," he'd say.

"Live for today," echoed my aunt. "You just never know."

"In the meantime," said Mother, shuffling the cards, "you have to live right."

Sid knocked on the wooden table. "Now, that's a fact."

In those dim, sweet, preconscious days, mortality was still remote, a rumor overheard from the province of adults. And as much as my father feared growing old—"Look at these gray hairs, Lil. They're a different texture altogether"—I believed that he was exempt from time, that his fears would never escalate, his wrinkles never deepen.

"At Cedars," groans my father as we pull into the parking lot, "they make me wait an hour and a half for my blood pressure medicine. Jeez, it makes me so mad I think I might get a heart attack right there. What's the stuff that you take, boychik? "

As we walk into Art's and wait to be seated for an early dinner, I tell my father about hydrochlorothiazide, proud that I can pronounce it, proud, even, that the pressure of our blood unites us. Swept up in a mood of camaraderie, of confidentiality, a mood intensified by the dim lighting, red walls, eclairs revolving in the pastry case, I share with my father the story of how, when I first took hydrochlorothiazide, I had a dream—my doctor warned me it might affect my dreams—in which I was fed glucose intravenously while being rolled down an alley on a gurney by a dozen identical Amazon women on roller skates who wore zebra-skin bikinis and told me they were taking me for an audience with their leader, a blind Las Vegas lounge singer, his pompadour oily and black.

My father is silent. He looks away. I panic that my story was inappropriate, that my father considers strange dreams a sign of instability, that I've made a fool of myself and put a dent in our burgeoning relationship.

"Dad," I say, blushing, "that drug is really strong the doctor said . . ."

"Prostate," shouts my father. The hostess looks up from her clipboard. Two blue haired women sitting in club chairs narrow their eyes. A man in Sans-A-Belt slacks peers in our direction. My father slaps his thigh and smiles. "They took out my prostate. I knew it would come to me sooner or later."

It's still eighty degrees out when we get back to my father's house. "How 'bout a swim?" he says. "I'll get the scuba gear. Ha ha."

"I don't have my trunks with me."

"So wear your underpants."

"Only if you do, too."

Father and I stand beside one another in boxer shorts, our toes hanging over the rim of the pool. Pine needles float on the surface of the water. A drowning bee flails in circles.

"You first," I say.

"What?" he says. He's taken out his hearing aid.

"I said, You first."

"You."

"You."

There has been, these summer evenings, a clear, incomparable cast of light, the air dry and slightly golden. It laves my father's pale body and he takes on that subtle strain of gold. Without his glasses, he cranes his face forward, eyes shining. The white hair on his chest and arms throws a profusion of tangled shadows. His belly protrudes like a little boy's. His knees are chapped and the skin is loose. His feet bear the ribbed impression of his socks.

"When you were just a baby," he says, gazing into the water, "you and your mom and I were out here, and she and I were talking, and we turned around and you were gone. Then Mother pointed at the pool. I swear you were down there, right on the bottom, blowing out bubbles, not crying or kicking, just looking up. Boy, was I scared, and I dove in and got you." My father looks at me. He puts his hand on my shoulder. "I don't suppose you remember that?"

"No," I say as he shoves me in the pool.

When I resurface, I see my father, arms outstretched, falling toward me, a look of blind abandon on his face. He hits the churning waves with a smack and springs up flinging water from his arms. He makes motor boat noises and plows his fist across the pool. He does an awkward handstand, skinny legs weaving through the air, hairs matted to calves. I'm in the deep end, treading water. "Look," he yells, turning profile. He dunks himself under, emerges with his cheeks full. He holds out his arms, hands bent back at a graceful angle, fingers splayed. A thin, silver jet of water shoots from the space between his two front teeth. It arches a yard in front of him, sputters and dwindles away.

"What am I?" he shouts, laughing and splashing.

"A fountain," I say, amazed.

Horseradish (Lessons in Pleasure and Pain)

I learned from my father that pleasure can merge with pain. The catalyst for my new knowledge was horseradish. Dad usually consumed it with Mother's boiled beef or gefilte fish, but in this instance it was eaten alone, directly from a condiment jar, with a tiny silver spoon. My father and I were squeezed into the breakfast nook, waiting for dinner, empty plates before us. The sun was going down; I looked out the kitchen window and tried to see the night happen. I must have worn the distant expression I was known for as a child. Even Mother's puttering—nibbling brisket, lifting lids—couldn't disrupt my concentration. I'm not sure when my hungry father inserted the spoon in his mouth. All I recall is the guttural noise, low at first, as though it came from outside the house, tugging me from my reverie. But the groan was deep in my father's throat, growing in volume, borne on the air, resounding in the room. And then I saw the silver spoon as he slid it out of his mouth.

My father knocked on his head with his fist, whined like a whistle, fanned his face. My father shuddered and pounded the table. His eyes were wide and red and wet from the sting of spice, the heat of the root. He gulped water to no avail. He sucked ice but that was futile. He tilted his head from side to side. Cartilage cracked. He blew his nose in a paper napkin. "God," he blurted, "is that ever good."

Mother turned from the stove and observed these antics with mild amusement. She shook her head. But something opened inside of me, some realization which, like my father's enjoyment, was burning and sweet at the same time. I couldn't think of any word for what I understood. Had I been pressed to describe it, I would have said that black and white can mix together, but remain black and white even though they make grey. There were, I sensed, other similar phenomena in the world: day and night, mother and father, happy and sad, in tandem and yet forever apart. Soon after that dinner, there followed several occurrences, featuring Father, which demonstrated the principle of pleasure hand in hand with pain.

The first involved the wrestler Gorgeous George. My father was a devout fan. Seated in a wing chair three feet away from our blond TV, he jumped up when George was victorious, cursed when George was pinned to the mat. If you watched my father on those Saturday nights, you'd think it was he who was being pummeled. He grabbed his throat during every half nelson, rolled with the blows when contenders were struck. He didn't, for a minute, believe that the competition was real. He knew that Gorgeous George—who wore a purple cape into the ring and primped his long, bleached hair—was coached to brag and flex and strut. And yet Father flinched and covered his eyes, yeowling in vicarious pain while his shoulders shook with laughter.

The second occurrence took place late one night on my way downstairs to get a glass of water. The rooms of the house were shot with moonlight cold as marble. Their door was ajar, their blanket heaving. A flash of my father's back. A glint of my mother's ring. Silence erupting with an utterance—his or hers I didn't know—that blended the sense of yes and no, the tones of yielding and protestation. And that was all, except for a snap of static when I touched the wrought-iron banister.

Though his doctor has given express instructions that my father avoid spicy food, he sometimes sneaks a dollop of horseradish. It may be the meager quantity that modifies his reaction. He may feel self-conscious at Art's Prime Rib, familiar as he is with the waitresses and waiters. Or perhaps the taste of horseradish has lost some of its zing. Whatever the reason, when my father scoops up a purple daub and touches it to his tongue, his eyes faintly water, his adam's apple bobs, the ghost of a smile shivers on his lips. "Yum," he says with brevity.

Before my father was married to Esther, he called me one night to ask for help. His voice was barely audible. Something about a pain in his side. I rushed to his house, letting myself in the front door with a key I hadn't used in years. I searched the rooms, calling and calling. I found him in pajamas, doubled up on the bathroom floor. His face was a knot. When he looked up, I felt I'd been struck by a gust of his pain.

I slid him into his pants and shirt, guiding his arms and spindly legs, softly repeating "There we go." When I buttoned him up, my face was inches away from his. I saw a collision of gratitude and shame that he worked his mouth to talk about. No sound came out. "You're fine," I said.

In the back seat of my car, headed for the emergency room—that's when the full hurt flooded his stomach. He clutched himself and called for God. I could see him in the rearview mirror, contorted and shining with sweat.

Later, after Dr. Henley diagnosed kidney stones, my father was tucked beneath a blanket and given a dose of Demerol. Together in a makeshift room—folding walls of gathered fabric—I held his hand, though I doubt he knew. Fluorescent light sputtered down like snow. His forehead grew cool. He tested words and slurred, his swallowing loud and dry. "Like having a baby. I couldn't bear . . ." and then he stared at the soundproof ceiling, the hundred holes like inverse stars. His muscles uncoiled and he breathed in relief. The pain that was building inside him became a portal my father stepped through.

As for pleasure, my father finds it these days in a prank, something he saw long ago in a movie, a prank he pulls when we dine together, a prank he never tires of; it makes him feel sly and quick and clever, proud he can make me break into laughter. Sylvie, the sixty-year-old hostess at Art's—a living mask of stiff hair, penciled eyebrows, crimson lips—grabs two leatherette menus as soon as she sees us coming. From behind a mahogany podium, Sylvie emerges in a knitted dress—

painted on, my father says—pink pastel with angora cuffs. "Boys," she coos, pivoting on a high heel, swinging her hips, "walk this way." And my father takes her literally, slinks behind her with tiny steps, head thrown back, hips liquid.

The Wind Did It

Jeopardy flickers on the wide-screen Zenith. The sound is down. My father is packing clothes for Samoa. Gauzy shirts, white trousers, plaid shorts. Using a method as complex as origami, he folds them into compact squares and pats them into the suitcase lying open on his bed. He moves with great deliberation, standing back to look at what he's packed as though he were painting a picture. He fills a shaving kit with mosquito repellent and suntan oil, and then he adds—just in case— Excedrin, cough drops, Band-Aids, Gas-X, Sudafed, and nasal spray.

I'm sprawled on my back in the middle of the room, picking at strands of plush carpet, wishing I hadn't eaten the cheesecake. But my father wanted to celebrate, to say good-bye with something sweet, and besides, he loves to watch me eat, especially foods his doctor forbids. I lift my head and lean on my elbow. "Say his name one more time."

"Muto Peli, the High Talking Chief of Samoa."

"What's that mean, the High Talking part?"

"He's like a spokesman sort of, an ambassador. I was his lawyer back when you were eight. Remember we took him to Disneyland? You didn't want to walk next to him because he wore mouse ears and a sarong. He laughed at everything—and I mean everything—and you told Mother he made you scared."

"How long's it been since you've seen him?"

"Jeez, twenty or something years. The last time I saw him was at a barbecue we had for him here. He drove women wild. The guy was fifty, at least, and fat. He roasted an entire pig on a spit; he'd dug a pit in the lawn, remember? And after we ate, he performed a farewell ceremony. Everyone was watching. He handed your mother and me a shell full of sap from the tappa root. It looked like glue, but sipping the stuff was a big honor. Mother went first. She held it in her mouth a long time, trying to muster the courage to swallow."

Suddenly I remember my mother, helpless surprise in her hazel eyes, lips clamped on the sour taste as she tried to force a grin. I also recall how, all my life, Mother flaunted her plans to leave. Every few months, for secret reasons, my mother threatened to move to the sea. "And honey," she'd tell me, "I'm taking you, too. We'll start our lives all over again. Wouldn't you love to live by the beach?" And often my father would disappear to Lancaster, Indio, Santa Rosa, away on business (he'd swear to my mother), returning with baskets of dried fruit wrapped in yellow cellophane. So relentless was their need to escape that during days of the Santa Anas, I'd imagine my parents walking out the door, swept in different directions by the wind, carried like blossoms on hot air, growing smaller and smaller.

"Samoa!" I say. "I can't believe you're really going."

My father flaps his wrinkled arms. "If I have to fly there myself."

We walk downstairs and out to my car. As we hug goodbye our glasses bump. I promise him I'll watch his house, water plants, collect the mail. I'm nervous like I used to be when he'd assign me something big to do and I wanted so badly to do it right I knew I'd do it wrong. Especially on Sundays when he gardened our yard, all grunts and curses and animal exertion. My mother and I would stay in the kitchen. She'd smoke a Lucky and stare into space while I colored at the breakfast table, keeping crayon within the lines. She seemed unaware of my father on those days, except that she'd wince when she heard his voice.

Otherwise she was far away, tanning on a stretch of sand. Eventually Father would bellow my name, demanding I get myself out of the house. I'd walk out the door and squint at the sun, waiting for instructions. The worst by far was coiling the hose, a task he claimed I could never do well, though he made me do it again and again. Heavy and green and recalcitrant, the hose would snake in the wrong direction and cramp with kinks I couldn't undo. When I was through it looked like a scribble, and my father would swear and shake his head, glaring at me long and hard, and I felt like nothing but skin and sweat.

Back at my own house, lying in bed, I read and reread the notes I wrote (what my father calls an "idiot list"): how and where to turn on the sprinklers, deactivate his burglar alarm. Moonlight seeps through my bedroom windows. A breeze begins to rattle the leaves. The air turns dry, its particles charged. Later that night when I awake, a neighbor's laundry is blowing off the line and lids from trash cans clatter through the street. Sirens are whining far away. I toss and turn as if on a spit, throw the blanket onto the floor. Though my father has only been gone a few hours, I decide I'd better check his house.

I can spot chartreuse a block away, and dim windows covered with bars. I park in the driveway and sit a minute. Thirty-two thousand one hundred three—the miles I've traveled in the past four years.

I don't bother to turn on the lights. I glide like a ghost from room to room, barely breathing, touching nothing. My heart is a wind chime spinning in my chest. The house is huge and solitary, all the furniture frosted with moonlight—couches, love seats, ottomans, wing chairs—big, sad, soft confections. Outside, the wind is tearing at the trees. Dogs bark in backyards.

Since Esther left, my father has used his dining-room table as a makeshift desk, eating lunch while he sorts the mail. I stand transfixed by the table's contents. He's hoarded coupons he'll never use—Scotchgard, Lime Away, Lady Clairol—torn from the Sunday *Times*. A yellowed brochure for a Mixmaster blender is open to the last page, its outdated warranty recently signed. There's an advertisement for ginseng capsules. A flyer for a missing child. A note that simply says *See you soon,* signed, *Rose—like the flower.*

These bits of paper he's sorted and stacked congeal into something definitive, final, an immense conception about my father that makes the concepts I'd formed in the past seem feeble and inadequate. And just as the fragments combine and cohere—his erratic love of women and money, his tantrums and dancing and banging blood, our season of feasting on prime rib—just as it all becomes seamless, complete, a branch crashes and breaks my concentration, I hear the wind scour the house.

"How was the chief?" I ask my father on the way to Art's. The Santa Anas still toss the trees.

"Fat as ever," my father says. "I've got slides to prove it. Samoan gals all over him like flies. I wish I could bottle that alteh kocker's secret."

"And the flight back, how was that?"

"Like a roller coaster at Coney Island. Thank God for Dramamine."

"Your plants?" I ask.

"Green as can be. But Bernard," he says, shifting in the seat, "something was wrong when I got back home."

My breath catches and lifts my ribs.

"Nothing's missing. Everything's there. But the front door was wide open."

"Oy," I gasp. "I'm *sure* I closed it." I'm really not sure but I say it twice. My face is hot. I try to fashion some excuse. I brace myself for a reprimand.

"It was kind of strange," my father says, gazing ahead, perfectly calm. "The door to the house just open like that. Anyone could've walked right in. Leaves and sunlight pouring through. It was fresh inside and . . . I don't know. Maybe, boychik, the wind did it."

A Pastoral Occasion

FRANKLIN BURROUGHS

FRANKLIN BURROUGHS grew up in South Carolina and now lives with his wife and children in Maine, where he teaches at Bowdoin College. He is the author of *Billy Watson's Croker Sack* (1991) and *The River Home: A Return to the Carolina Low Country* (1993).

We at last decided to make an end to things, and put Jacob down. You put an old dog down to abbreviate his suffering or free yourself of his inconvenience.

He is thirteen, his birthday falling within a month of Elizabeth's. He can scarcely rise unassisted—each morning he looks like a man trying to pull an overturned wagon. Nothing wrong with his forelegs—he is a massive, deep-chested dog. But the hips, congenitally defective, have grown steadily worse. The atrophied thighs lie awkwardly out to the side as he heaves himself up. Then he pulls ahead, his toenails scrabbling against the floor, until the wasted hindquarters trail out behind him. Now he can slowly curl them beneath him, into something like a sitting posture, from which, panting, tottering, he rises. There is no triumph in it. He looks at us with the hangdog look of apology, supplication, and fear.

Age is a terror. He senses the impatience with which we, busy people with things to do, wait on each labored ascension, so that we may let him out in the morning and in the evening. Worse than his mortification is his humility. He wags his hindquarters as short-tailed dogs do, writhing in gratitude. It is the hideous smile of a very old, very infirm man. It proclaims his daily knowledge that he has outlived nature, and must trust to the uncertainties of our forbearance. He has lived like this for two years. But we cannot appease age, and he grows slowly weaker. Any least thing trips him—the threshold of a door, a child's shoe.

He is grizzled, his old muzzle almost white, gone gaunt and surprisingly soft, like threadbare corduroy. His eyes, milky with cataracts, are reptilian. Strange wrinkled tumors—benign, Harry Ahern has told us—sprout from his underside and along one flank, like misplaced nipples or bloated wood ticks. When Bonnie first came into the house last year, as a six-week-old weanling puppy, she would sometimes tug at them. He would growl, and once snapped hard at her, with a speed and savagery that surprised us all. Bonnie scampered under the stove, yowling with terror, and he looked up, whimpering, contrite, thumping his stump of tail on the floor, acknowledging that he had no right to do it, no right at all. Please forgive again, please once more.

There is more to it. He stinks. His flatulence has become legendary, his breath an abomination. But the worst is a sourness connected to no bodily process, that emanates from his coat, from the whole rickety carcass he has dragged through these last years of his life. Bathing does little good; the smell overrides even the pleasant, cleanly fragrance of the soap. The stink of mortality does not wash out, scrub and scour it as you will. Even our youngest daughter shuns him, out of some instinct deeper than fastidiousness.

But his appetite, the most reliable of a dog's vital indicators, is undiminished. If anything, it is greater than it was in his prime. He sees little more than shadows, but knows the routines of the house completely. He can tell at once if I am angry, although he cannot tell why, and blames himself, cringing and fawning. He knows by the rhythm of traffic through the kitchen when we are leaving on a trip, and hauls himself under the stove, miserable, waiting to be dragged out and taken to the kennel. Such a dog has no difficulty in knowing when it is suppertime, and he will not be put off or placated. At five o'clock he gets up and dogs me, stands in my way, pushes his snout against my leg, until I get his pan. Then his ears lift up, his old eyes gleam with a muddy lambency, and his breath comes in harsh, hoarse gasps. He is underfoot as we go out to the barn and fill the pan; he has his muzzle in it before it touches the floor. His sides heave as he eats. If Bonnie is dilatory or momentarily distracted from her food, he is in her bowl in an instant. Normally the most obedient of dogs, he cannot be called off, and I must grab him by the scruff and lift his head out of the dish, his jaws still working. It is somehow obscene, too much like the cold vision of Death as a skeleton whose hunger is never glutted, or a parody of all the unseemly desires that stay with us, long after we should have satisfied or subdued them. Increase of appetite growing by what it feeds on, ravening the devourer.

We are in late summer, the world green and gracious, the fields new mown and studded with big cylindrical bales like tumuli, and the young swallows, fledged now, gathering by dozens, by scores, and at last by hundreds on the wires, skimming out low over the fields, returning, with their squeaky cries, their sudden restlessness. Crickets sing in the stubble at dusk. Our children are healthy, the youngest never more so. She is full of talk and jokes, proudly displays her own small garden of radishes, which prosper, and flowers, plucked the moment they blossom. But there is also the evening news, which this summer revives images of Hiroshima and the Holocaust, and those images, from which no one, no matter how deep in the country, is free, loom out at us again—the sunken eyes and faces, the piled bodies, arms and legs akimbo, waxy white, soft as wax. Victims of the famine in Ethiopia merge with these, at some level below thought; they too stare out, too numbed to brush away the flies that batten on starvation. My children gaze at children whose bellies are taut and round as the swelled throats of the toads that trill around our doorstep each evening.

Meanwhile, we eat well, fresh healthy things from the garden, occasionally a mackerel or bluefish from the teeming summer sea. But our eldest daughter renounces the eating of flesh and flirts—just to scare herself, she says—with anorexia. Between meals she slips into the pantry and stands there, gorging on crackers or potato chips, pressing them by the handful into her mouth. The dog in our midst is not a figure from an allegory, or, if so, from the allegory that also contains ourselves. To get into the pantry, we must shove his heavy bulk aside, making room for the door to swing open.

Great schools of menhaden, driven by voracious bluefish, have crowded their way upriver. It happens each summer. Soon there are too many fish trying to feed and flee and breathe; too much blood and flesh clouding the water after each new onslaught; too little oxygen. Fish—predators and prey—die by the thousands. It is no cause for alarm, a fisheries biologist announces; indeed, it is a sign of the restored health of the river that it occasionally chokes and gags on its own fecundity this way. For Bonnie, it is a boon. She finds dead fish along the tide-line, and rolls in them ecstatically until her coat gleams with scales and tallowy fish grease. She reeks proudly, and cocks her tail with a new jauntiness. Jacob sniffs and licks her as though she were in heat: a seedy, broken-down roué, paying the homage of his creaking gallantry to a fine-fleshed young woman, perfumed, made-up, and ready for an evening's patrolling and prospecting along the boulevards. Ourselves caricatured in canine drag, the mirror nature holds up to our most unnatural extravagances.

Susan and the girls would go over to Bremen on Wednesday, to spend a week with her parents. She would be joined there by her cousin and his family—prodigal Martin, who ten years ago left college and fled New England for the Northwest Territory, and who returned last year, with a wife and two children. His father had died in the interval, and he now assumed, effortlessly and unexpectedly, his father's role within the family—healer, restorer, with a gift for releasing the family's impacted and complex affections. His returns, like his father's, have never been long enough or often enough, and they call for the fatted calf, an undeclared, impromptu Thanksgiving. I would join them on Saturday, but first planned for myself two days of fishing up north, on the Penobscot.

We talked it all out on Tuesday. Jacob would never survive another winter. His joints stiffened and grew more painful each year as the cold began to creep into the house. He was becoming incontinent, and could not reliably contain himself at night. Whatever fond memories we might have of the dog were disappearing fast, consumed by what he had become. This would be the time for it. We would not tell the children beforehand. No need for them to know that the old dog, sleeping as usual, whimpering fretfully in his sleep, would die that afternoon. Let them have only their own happiness to consider on Wednesday morning, with the prospect of the drive over to Bremen, then the swimming in the cold, salty tide pond there, and seeing the cousins and grandparents again. If they knew, they would suddenly try to see him, as you try to see familiar places or people when you are about to leave them for good. Their caresses and expiatory attentions, hugs, pats, tears, would only trouble him. I wished to spare them, and myself, their grief. In proportion to their age, it would be less self-conscious, less corroded by the knowledge that it would quickly pass, that it had not been earned by earnest love, that it was adulterated by that generalized pity which is finally self-pity. Hannah's would be Eden-grief—natural tears easily shed, and soon wiped. Elizabeth would know more, and Coles yet more, of the pretense that infects even our most spontaneous sorrows. Out of sight, out of mind would prevail in the end, so let the sleeping dog lie this morning in sight but out of mind, as he had lain for so many mornings before.

On Wednesday we ate our breakfast. I kissed them goodbye, and went in for a morning in the office. It was a productive morning; my mind was not on the dog. He impinged on my concentration only as the consciousness of something unpleasant—*what was it? O yes. That*—to be done in the afternoon. At noon, I went home and fixed lunch. He pulled himself up and came over, not to be patted but to sniff me thoroughly. Mostly blind, surrounded by the gibberish of human voices, he takes the world in through his nose. As I sat to eat, he barked his stentorian, concussive bark, demanding to be let out. I let him out. As I sat again, he barked again, demanding to be let in. I let him in. This was repeated twice before I had finished my sandwich. He reminds you of someone looking for something mislaid, growing frantic, passing from one room to the next and back again, not sure, after a while, of where he has or has not searched, even of where he is. Jacob's insistence is maddening when this fit seizes him. If you are slow in responding to his bark, he will paw at the door latch with his great forepaw, gouging the wood with his nails. No door in our house he cannot eventually open, no door unscoured by his foot. Often we hear him at night—the steady rasp, rasp of the paw at the door and at last, by blind chance and mindless persistence, the click of the latch and the creaking open of the door.

It was hot. I napped briefly after lunch, then got back up. He was sound asleep when I went out. I shut Bonnie in her pen, got a shovel, and walked across the stubble, to where the pasture slopes down to the river. In the days when the town, and all New England, were intensively farmed, this slope too had been mown and kept, but that had been many years ago. Now chokecherry, viburnum, sumac, and hawthorne had sprung up, and the remaining bits of pasture grass were disappearing under thistle and goldenrod. At the edge of the swampy border between the slope and the river were posted a few knobby apple trees, clogged with dead wood. Slowly, year by year, they were being taken by the alders that crept up from the swamp. They still bore fruit, sparsely or abundantly according to some rhythm of their own, which seemed largely unrelated to the vagaries of the season. The apples were small and of a palate-withering sourness, but grouse loved them, especially once they were softened by the first lethal frosts of October.

I picked a clearing on the slope, where there would be no roots to contend with, removed the sod, and began to dig. Graves are traditionally long and narrow, but a shovel, by the curvature of its blade, wants to dig a round hole. It had been a dry summer, and the soil—the notorious blue clay of Bowdoinham—grew harder as I dug down. Three feet would do for a dog, I told myself—but a full three feet, an honest three feet. A foot below the surface, the clay assumed a consistency almost like shale; it came up in shards and curled shavings. This slowed the work, but pleased me: the shovel carved out walls as clean and definite as the inner walls of an unglazed pot. The blade clinked and scraped in the still heat of early afternoon. When the circular hole was too deep for me to use my foot against the shoulder of the shovel blade, I rammed it down with both hands, again and again, as you would a posthole digger. My hole now had its shape and depth—round, narrower at the top than at the bottom, where, as best I could, I hollowed out a chamber. Jacob would lie in a cavity the shape of an urn or uterus.

None of this was necessary. I might have taken him to the vet's, scratched him behind the ears, and left him there. He had been left there often enough not to be alarmed by it. Harry would do the rest, and dispose of him afterwards. If we wished, he could even arrange for the dog to be cremated. He had given me a booklet explaining such things, called *Parting with Your Pet*. That would be the painless and convenient way to do it, and it was not clear to me why I felt it could not be done that way, since he was dying precisely for the sake of painlessness and convenience. But for the moment the satisfaction of digging the grave seemed solid enough. Deerflies troubled me some; cicadas buzzed, and my eyes blurred with sweat. A killdeer called out from the deep abyss of the August sky. It was hard to think beyond the job at hand, which I now finished. I stood to admire it for a moment, and then walked back up to the house.

There was time for a swim in the river, at the town landing. I went there, dived in, and swam up against the tide a long way, well on toward exhaustion, and drifted lazily back down. That just left time enough to change clothes, pick up the dog, put him into the truck, and drive briskly into town. Harry wanted to do it last thing before he closed for the afternoon. Perhaps this was for the sake of his customers. Even if it is only your canine or feline proxy, and not yourself, you do not like to be reminded that some patients enter hospitals for the purpose of dying.

I left him in the back of the truck. Harry's office is a remodeled house at the edge of town, and he keeps the grounds neatly groomed— petunias line the gravel walkway; cosmos and daisies bloom in the mulched beds that flank the front door. Inside, everything is linoleum and vinyl, but the sense of homeyness is preserved by the two or three friendly assistants who work with Harry each summer. Some are already through veterinary school and are serving a kind of internship; others are just beginning and are gaining early experience in what they plan to be their life's work. Mostly, they are young women, both dedicated and cheerful, good at putting animals and their owners at ease. Harry himself is that way—relaxed, sympathetic, with an air of professional discretion. He has grown himself a fine, full beard, which he keeps carefully trimmed, to emphasize a certain scholarly quality in him. Vets are no longer horse doctors, obstetricians to cows and ewes, gelders of boars and bulls. Their clients are mostly suburban; they are pet doctors, with a professional personality like that of a good pediatrician.

I watched with some amusement as Harry finished with his next-to-last customer of the day, a lady in sandals and sunglasses, who held a groggy, post-operative tomcat in her arms. Post-operative and post-tom too, I gathered. He was assuring her that the cat would hold nothing against her. She plainly doubted him: "Won't he always feel I've deprived him of something?" Harry said no, not at all. The cat would only suffer from a little local discomfort for a couple of days. After that, he'd be as happy as a clam at high tide. She left, holding the cat close to her face, nuzzling it. Harry had once studied to be a priest, and I considered a bad joke, a way to lighten the moment—"So now he's the involuntary Origen of his species." But Harry was busy, his back to me, as he placed a few things quickly, almost furtively, into a narrow black case. He said something to the receptionist about tomorrow's appointments and turned abruptly, with a kind of brusqueness, to me. "Let's go," he said.

It all went quickly now. I lowered the tailgate and crawled up inside the truck. Jacob was trying to rise. I helped him up, and he walked to the edge of the tailgate, his spine humped, his tail wagging the equivalent of the uncertain smile with which you approach a person who may choose not to recognize you. Harry was looking at him, then looked at me. "It's time to do it all right," he said, allowing no second thoughts. It was easy to get the dog to lie down on the tailgate and keep still. I squatted beside him, and rubbed his ears and nape. Harry opened his case, took out a rubber tube, wrapped it around the fore-leg, tightened and knotted it. He drew a clear liquid into the syringe, found the vein with his forefinger, and slipped the needle in. An inky spurt of blood, curling and roiled like smoke, appeared in the syringe. Then the slow pressure of the thumb on the plunger. forcing first the blood back into the vein, then the anesthetic. Thirteen years of life fig-ured in that small action—the jet of living blood into the clear fluid, the squeezing of blood and fluid back into the dog.

There was no convulsion or shudder. Almost as soon as the plunger started forward, the dog's breathing grew easy and unlabored. His eyes closed, and the breathing became steadily deeper and more de-liberate. When the plunger was something more than half advanced, he sighed profoundly, as though after a very good meal, and stopped breathing. Harry completed the injection, withdrew the needle, and leaned forward to lift the dog's eyelid with his thumb—a deft, sacer-dotal motion. He seemed satisfied with what the eye contained, but drew some more fluid into the syringe. "He's a big fellow," he said. "We'd better play it safe. A bouncy truck ride can act as artificial re-spiration." I nodded because I could not trust my throat to speak. He picked up the limp foreleg, offhandedly this time, jabbed the needle in, and emptied it quickly.

When I got down from the tailgate and looked up, the day seemed very bright, as though I had emerged from a cinema in midafternoon. I started to walk back toward the office with Harry, to pay the bill, but he touched my shoulder. "Don't bother. We'll mail it in the morning."

I nodded again, and for some reason shook his hand, and returned to the truck.

As I drove home, I found it possible to remember beyond Jacob's decrepitude, back to when he had been a valued dog. It was not like the breaking of a dam—there was no sudden flood of recollections and images. It was rather as though a blocked passage or interrupted circuit had been cleared, restoring normal communication. Memory follows certain forms and conventions—the obvious one of chronology, the less obvious ones that edit your remembering and fit it to a theme. A dog is not complex—dogs are what they are from a very early date. They do not change, and if they surprise you, it is probably because you have been inattentive. But our gift for complicating our relation to the simplest things is endless, even when we have selected those things in the hope that they might simplify our selves. The dog was part of the life I had chosen, with the faith that it might somehow educate me, lead me out of myself toward a solid world, where things existed, and might be experienced without reflection.

Hunting is an ancient metaphor for this active, unreflective life, for desire in the unheeding pursuit of its object. That is, it is a metaphor for a life in which nothing is metaphoric, and which need not imagine itself in any other terms. But I had always owned hunting dogs—pointers, like Jacob, or brittanies or setters—and at some point I noticed that all of them were neurotic, and that this was because of what was expected of them. Their instinct to hunt, to track, stalk, seize, and kill, was simultaneously fostered and frustrated. The dog was always denied the last gratification: it was to point, but not to pounce, to seize the downed bird, but not to devour it. Before Jacob, every hunting dog I owned, good or bad, had had a certain air of hysteria,

of pent-up energy that would periodically explode, and render it un-
manageable for an hour, or even an entire afternoon of swearing and
storming and cajoling. Hunter and dog on such occasions become trite
illustrations of superego and id, repressive dictatorship and anarchic
mob, each the agent of the other's frenzy. So not even hunting dogs,
much less their owners, abandoned themselves to headlong pursuit of
the object. When they did, it was something like insanity.

Jacob had none of this. I had picked him from a squirming litter and
brought him home. We named him Jacob because his coat—dingy
white heavily spotted and ticked with brown—resembled the variety of bean called Jacob's cattle. There had been a jar of them on the
kitchen counter when I brought him into the house, and we had
looked at the dog, then at the jar, and it had seemed, in a minor way, a
sign—here was the obvious name for a puppy who needed one, and
who still had the plump shapelessness of a beanbag. Driving home
now, I found that time present and available to me as it had not been
even an hour before. Elizabeth, not yet two weeks old, lay upstairs
in her hamper. Susan's sewing basket was on the kitchen table, filled
with scraps of colorful material intended for an infant's quilt. She had
hoped to finish it before the baby was born, and felt determined to
finish it now, so that Elizabeth might have what you would like each
child to have—some labor of love to lie in, something bright and soft
to greet its awakening to the world. The puppy whimpered some
that first night, and we could hear a certain amount of bumping and
scraping from the kitchen, where we had left him in a large box.
Next morning we found him out of the box, beside the overturned
sewing basket, bedded down in the quilt scraps. He looked at us, his
brow furrowed with uncertainty, as though he expected a scolding.
Susan laughed—"Maybe we should name you Joseph, with your coat

of many colors, and pack you off to Egypt—maybe that's what we'd better do. Is that what you'd like?"

But he remained Jacob, after the clever and conniving supplanter whom he did not particularly resemble. Before he was three months old, it was apparent that his hips were bad, and we had to decide whether or not to keep him. He was brighteyed and endearing, already housebroken, and so we kept him. I felt a misgiving about this, the way you do when you yield to your own tenderheartedness. The hunters I had known in my boyhood doted on their dogs and treated them well, but they would have put down a genetically imperfect one as unhesitatingly as they would have returned a piece of defective merchandise, and with the same sense that their doing so was *pro bono publico* and not merely for themselves. I went ahead and trained him, and we hunted for all but his last two years, despite his progressive infirmity. He was, from the beginning, a melancholy, conscience-stricken dog, with no instinct for play or mischief. It goes without saying that, even in his old age, the sight of the gun and hunting coat excited him, and set him into a geriatric capering around the truck, waiting to be lifted in. But once afield, he was always careful, worried and tentative, as though he suspected a booby trap at every turn. My least show of exasperation demoralized him, and he would simply sit, as though commanded to do so, and refuse to hunt. So I learned to say nothing at all that might inhibit him, and he would move ahead of me with great diffidence, looking back inquiringly every few yards, like a batter checking with the third base coach after each pitch. He had no style at all; he looked like something you might see slinking among overturned garbage cans in an alleyway.

At home, even as a young dog, he was inclined to lie low, and he confined himself to an imaginary kennel that he created in the corner of the kitchen between the stove and the pantry. He seldom left it voluntarily, clinging to it as stubbornly as some of us cling to our self-imposed limitations. The children accepted him as children accept the given circumstances of their lives, and he tolerated them in the same way. But unfamiliar children filled him with consternation, and he would retreat from their overtures into the darkest corner of the kitchen and cower there, growling, his eyes baleful, his tail clapped between his legs. Our friends regarded him as the expression of a self-consciously quirky taste, like a stuffed moose head over the mantel or a pair of plaster flamingos on the lawn, and as an invitation to wit. It became a joke to name him; he was Lazarus, Tithonus, Aeolus of the ill wind, the grim sleeper, Uriah Heep; Cotton Mather and a giraffe were implicated in his ancestry. When company came for supper, he would bark at each new arrival with the implacability of an unattended moralist, and eventually edge up to each person in turn, and sniff suspiciously, and then, his worst expectations confirmed, he would retreat to his corner. There he would sleep loudly, his snoring filling the intervals of conversation. Occasionally I would look over and see him, still tightly curled in his corner, his back to the room, but awake now, his head lifted just enough to glare at me with one reproachful eye. Then he would sigh, shift a little, and resume his sleep. He was like an old family retainer or a poor relation, some vestige of your earlier circumstances, never allowing you to forget that he knew his place, and asserting his rights by denying that he had any. But he was quiet and reclusive, seldom much of a nuisance.

Hunting was in October, for grouse. They seemed so deeply indigenous to this part of New England that, in hunting them, I felt myself at times infringing on a privilege properly belonging only to natives. Their fondness for apples explains why they haunt old house sites, farms sunk back into forest, and the stone fences that once marked the borders of fields. Further north, they are a true forest bird, but here they have become a bird of abandoned history, as though they had once been domestic fowl, left to fend for themselves when the families moved on to richer lands along the primeval Ohio, or when the young men did not return from Chancellorsville or the Seven Days, Little Round Top or the Bloody Salient. You imagine the birds clinging hard to the deserted farmstead for as long as anything was there—pecking in the earth where the garden was, scratching beneath the rotting sills of the barn for whatever grain had sifted through, filling their gizzards with grit from the road while the road lasted, until slowly the sumacs edged into it, and the alders, and it ceased to be a road. But—sometimes in regular orchards, but much more commonly planted thriftily along stone fences or at the edge of fields, or on the banks of gullies too steep to mow—the apple trees persisted, renewed themselves, and kept bearing, and the grouse haunted them, elusive and shadowy as fugitives.

A more energetic and exuberant dog would have been an intruder in these places. Jacob was as discreet and somber as an undertaker. Grouse are unalterably wild, and will not hold for a dog as quail or woodcock do. In the thick, overgrown country, you seldom had more than a fleeting glimpse of one, a blurred impression of wings. No matter how diligent the dog, most of our hunts ended without a shot being fired. This did not bother me. I liked the places the birds took us. Looking into an old cellar hole, where a sturdy ash had thrust its way up through the chimney arch, or peering down into the cool, reverberant depths of a well, I had the sense of a history much older than was in fact the case, as though I had been a citizen of the later empire, who had come upon some solid, incontrovertible vestige of the early republic, of a past long since digested into nostalgia and literature. The morose, painstaking dog faded into this scene as a fish dissolves from your sight back down into deep water, and I followed the thin clinking of his collar tags as best as I could.

As he got older and slower, he became more and more effective. Certain trees had a special attraction to grouse, even in years when they were not bearing well, and each of these was a problem to be solved, an approach to be worked out, the dog coming in from one side, perhaps, and the hunter standing off in a small clearing to the other side, in hopes that the bird would flush that way, and afford a shot. The odds still favored the bird, but not so extravagantly as they had done. The dog was methodical, and he knew each place as well as he knew the kitchen, the barn, the yard, and absolutely nothing else. I seldom spoke to him, or whistled him in, or told him his business. He never overran a bird, or failed to find a dead one. Slowly, October after October, I came to feel almost naturalized, if not to the region and the town, then at least to these few bypassed, unvisited spots, where particular apple trees stood and created small clearings in the forest. I could distract insomnia by visualizing each of the four or five farms we hunted regularly, and recalling, individually, each of the birds we had taken there. At some point I realized that he was easily the best hunting dog I had ever owned, but I could hardly boast about him, as he lay curled in his usual corner of the kitchen, as indifferent to our comings and goings as a mule would have been.

By his tenth year, he could not walk a mile without resting, and so we began to hunt by driving as close as possible to the most reliable trees, checking them quickly, and driving on to the next farm and the next tree. This altered our hunting, by depriving the places of their context. It was not exactly like reading an abridged version of a book, or seeing only the most eventful innings of a game; it was more like what happens when you stop trying to remember people or events in their fullness, and content yourself with recalling them as they appear in snapshots, or as they are preserved in some oft-repeated anecdote. But we killed grouse at an unprecedented rate that October. It was Nimrod's daydream, the dog flawless, the bird always at the expected place, the gun unable to miss. Again and again there would be the abrupt explosion of the flush, the shadowy instant when the gun finds the bird even before the mind has registered its image, and then, with no consciousness of having released the safety or pulled the trigger, the bird falling, the solid thump against the ground that makes it real. Jacob would fetch it as he always did, not mangling it or even disturbing its feathers, but powerfully reluctant to let go until I gave his ear a tug, which caused him to drop it abruptly, as though it were hot. The limp weight and dry, dusty smell of the bird were magically accomplished facts, and there would, by a different kind of magic, be a bird in the same place when we returned to it the following week. At the end of the season, I drew a rough map of each of our regular territories, and marked on each map the places where we had gotten grouse, and the date. They had become too many for me to rehearse to myself at night, trying to put myself to sleep. His life's work came to forty-six grouse. There were a good many more woodcock—too many to bother with—but they were only incidental.

By the next October he could scarcely go a hundred yards before his legs gave out. I took him out once, to a woodcock cover close beside the road, but he could not manage even that, so I returned him to the truck and started home. On the way, or not much out of the way, there was a favored apple tree, one of our regular spots. I left him whimpering and barking in the truck. A grouse was there, but it flushed out of range. Walking back to the truck through a cutover area, I flushed and killed a woodcock. It fell into a pile of slash, and search as I might I could not find it. It ended with my going back to the truck, picking up the dog, and lugging him across the logging debris to where the bird had fallen. He smelled it even before I put him down on the slash pile, and, after a moment of noisy rooting and snuffing, he extricated the bird. I put it in my coat, lugged him back to the truck, then returned and got the gun, and that was our last hunt.

From then on he lay, twelve months a year instead of eleven, in the kitchen, beside the stove in summer, under it in winter, struggling up only to eat and to go outside off and on during the day, in his fitful, distracted way, as though looking for something missing. We got Bonnie, an affable young retriever. In the coldest weather the two of them curled into a single lump of dog. He exhibited no jealousy. His eyes faded, although he knew so well, by smell and habit, the kitchen, the barn, and the dooryard, that this seldom inconvenienced him. I only realized how blind he had become one day when he walked squarely into a little wagon that Hannah had left on the back step. It alarmed him, and he sat down and barked at the thing, dogmatic, querulous, not to be placated—a Job whose patience this last small indignity, added to his life's list of afflictions, had broken.

I drove the truck past the house, across the pasture, and to the edge of the slope. The last strong afternoon light fell nearly horizontal across the stubble, the shadow of the house stretched far into the field. The slope itself lay in deep shadow now. Grief, the swelling of the throat and blurring of the eyes, is involuntary, and it is pointless to try to decide when circumstances do or do not justify it. But it surprised me all the same. I opened the tailgate. He lay in a posture resembling sleep, but with the limbs and angle of the head wrong, somehow too slack and lax. It looked like a competent amateur's rendering of a dog—the proportions right, the legs and ears and muzzle all accurately done, and yet no sense of the whole thing as one creature. It was awkward lifting him. His dead weight shifted like sand in a sack, and he was a heavy animal. I had to put him down on his back and drag him by the forelegs the last few yards.

I tried to lower him gently, but he slipped free and flopped down into the grave with a sodden thud. And with that he sighed and grunted softly. It was unmistakable. I felt a kind of horror. Had the truck ride, and this final bump, revived him? It took a certain clench-jawed deliberation not to shovel the dirt down on him immediately, or simply turn and walk away. I made myself watch him closely for what I did not want to see—some fluttering of the eyelid or flexing of the nostril. Nothing seemed to move, but it was dark in the hole, and the signs of life would be very dim. I knelt to peer in more closely, and finally reached my hand down to touch him, as gingerly as you might touch an iron to see if it were hot. The air was dank and chill beneath the earth, but his flank still felt warm. There was no respiration. I pressed the heel of my hand hard against his rib cage. He sighed. So that was all—the fall had forced air from his lungs, as from a bellows. I withdrew my arm and looked at him again. He lay awkwardly, his limbs sprawled, like a dead dog beside the road. I reached back down, turned him on his side, and drew the legs into the curled position natural to any animal at rest. He looked comfortable now, an accurate representation of a sleeping dog.

Impossible not to think of him as he had lain for so many years in his corner, while doors opened and shut, friends entered and left, and the children, growing up, began to come and go. I slowly began shoveling the dry, rubbly clay back into the hole, covering him gradually, moving forward from the hindquarters. When he lay under a blanket of dirt, with only his head and shoulders visible, I looked at him a last time, then looked no more, and shoveled methodically until the grave was filled and mounded. When I stopped, it was suddenly cool in the shadows, and you could feel how the year was turning away toward autumn; but high overhead a few bland clouds still drifted in a placid summer sky. We might set up a stone later, but this would do for now.

A Day at the Beach

GEOFFREY WOLFF

GEOFFREY WOLFF is the author of a number of important books of nonfiction, including *A Day at the Beach* (1992) and *The Duke of Deception: Memories of my Father* (1979), the autobiographical account of his childhood. He lives in Jamestown, Rhode Island.

I'd be the last one to brag up my vacation, show slides of Mustique's Cotton Club, Curtain Bluff you, Bitter End you, call Petit St. Vincent by its initials (PSV). As for chit-chatting my physiological bona fides, my regime, pulse rate at rest, systolic upper (let's talk through the roof), and diastolic lower (shoot the moon), my SGOT abnormalities, the uric acid settled in gouty crystals at my extremities—would I impose the particulars?

But to reveal both beach and body: here reticence yields to candor. All too soon you'll know of Sint Maarten and cardiac catheterization of La Samana and acute aortic valvular stenosis, of the Wolff Family Christmas, of surgical procedures, of the very heart of me.

Not long ago I flew with my family from New York to Antigua. The jumbo jet was full, and occupied principally (my two teenage sons noticed) by people old enough to drive but young enough not to know what is an IRA. These travelers smiled and had good teeth. I was old enough (then) to have all the friends I wanted, but my sons had another perspective, and they smiled back. Until we descended to Sint Maarten, our stopover, ten flying minutes from Antigua. The airplane unloaded every person with perfect white teeth, leaving us to fellow passengers plenty old enough to know their 401(k) retirement strategies. Golfers, hatched from madras eggs.

Oh, my poor boys! They pressed their noses to the Boeing's windows and watched the smiling young people skip toward Sint Maarten's terminal.

"We'll visit Sint Maarten someday," their mummy promised, calling it "Saynt Martin."

Not so fast! By June, all seats had been booked to that island for that Christmas vacation. I tried to pull strings, making my way up a chain of command to an executive of one of our most venerable international airlines. He wished to serve, but I heard in his voice a quality I couldn't then put a name to; I think I could now, if only I knew the exact antonym for "ballyhoo": would it be "demotion"? Perhaps "derision"? He suggested Jamaica. How about Barbados? Why not try Trinidad? He boosted other islands, to which his airline did not fly. For a fellow with almost as much experience living well as I had of living, I wasn't hearing the music.

We would go to Sint Maarten, by God, and so, with a sigh, the airline executive accommodated us.

An alarm bell rang a few days before takeoff during a phone talk with my mother, who had on some dreamy caprice visited during a single journey every Caribbean island with an airport, and some without, returning thereafter to none.

"Saint Martin?" my mother said, "or Sint Maarten?"

"What's the difference?"

"Sint Maarten is the Dutch part. Saint Martin is French. The French have fun, and eat good food."

"Our destination is Sint Maarten," I said.

"Oh," my mother said. "Huh."

"What do you mean, 'huh,'" I asked.

"Well," my mother said.

"Did you not care for the island?" I asked.

"Well," my mother said, "it has beaches. The French part. Or it did when I was there."

"Why would the beaches not be there now?"

"Oh, the construction. There were buildings going up all along the beaches."

"Pretty buildings?"

"I think I liked San Juan a little more than Saint Martin," my mother said.

"Did you like San Juan?"

"Not at all," my mother said. "It was tacky."

I concluded that Sint Maarten might be just the place for my sons, and I felt virtuous thinking this, the way St. Sebastian must have felt when the arrows came.

Travelogues and medical logs first intersect at Theodore Francis Green Airport, Providence, Rhode Island, 6:15 A.M., Saturday, mid-December. I am famously efficient, dependable. I use the old noodle, pack early, remember to bring tickets, passports, extra eyeglasses, maps to be studied en route, the novel by Dostoyevski I have still not read, medication—*all* the necessaries. These I arrange in a canvas briefcase, and leave it in our driveway. Priscilla, for a wonder, had taken upon herself responsibility for the tickets and passports, so we were not grounded. But I was destined to fly away without my drugs. This was the conventional pharmacopoeia of a fellow of late-middle years: Benemid and colchicine (gout), Vasotec (hypertension), Inderal (heart rate). I didn't like flying to an island, at the beginning of a weekend, without these medicines: a general practitioner in our little town had a few days before, during my first visit with him, expressed quiet alarm at my blood pressure. I had visited him because, seized by a fitness fit, I had labored several months to row nowhere fast, and the more often I pulled on the handle of that Concept II Ergometer, the very machine favored by Olympic oarsmen, the less my stamina. My older son, Nicholas, can row the unmoved contraption more than twenty miles, and take a telephone call, and talk. I'd row three and double over. This didn't seem fair; it wasn't fair, my new doctor agreed, asking by the way did I know I had a heart murmur. I told him I had been told this since childhood, but it was nothing, it had been checked out.

"Checked out how?"

I explained, perhaps condescendingly, that in the metropolis of Providence I had not three years before been tested hi-tech with an echocardiogram, and the results had shown I had the heart of a baby. Those were my city doctor's very words, I explained, "heart of a baby." My new doctor said very well, but my blood pressure must be diminished medically and, by the way, might he send away for those echocardiogram test results, just to see them, satisfy his curiosity about the clamorous mutter he had heard listening to my heart?

Just before and after this physical examination I had been preoccupied with photographs, arranging the slides and prints of twenty-one years of marriage and nineteen years of daddydom in albums, to give as Christmas gifts to my kin. I am obsessive, but in the process of finding and sorting these pictures of a life, likenesses of my father and mother, their fathers and mothers, this innocent labor radiated out and became even by my tolerant lights weird, alarming. I dropped business and pleasure to sort, hunting through trunks and cartons in the attic several nights till dawn. Priscilla, whom I had meant to surprise pleasantly with photographs of herself, asked what I thought I was doing. Meaning to answer truthfully, I said I didn't really know.

"I'm arranging things," I said. "It's as though I think I'm about to die," I said.

"I don't find that amusing," she said.

"I don't either," I said.

In truth, I think I thought no such thing. I didn't imagine dying, or didn't imagine dying any more often than I usually do, which isn't that often. But I'd felt *something*, and it had sent me to trunks in my attic and to a doctor, who urged me to take my medicine.

Flying to Sint Maarten I considered Vasotec. Landing at Sint Maarten, Saturday afternoon, I brooded on Benemid. I am not famously even-tempered; our bags, minus the carry-on of essentials snowed under in our driveway, were delayed. It seemed to me, elbowing through throngs to the baggage carousel, that I was being elbowed back. Irritable, I felt a bellicose rush of blood to my face; I was showing my fighting colors.

Our taxi was no jitney daubed pastel but a businessman's sedan; the driver was all business, no *Welcome to de Islands, mon*, but "Where to?"

We told him where. He seemed amused. Leaving the airport, he turned left and drove beside a chain-link fence bordering the runway. Left again, beside a fence bordering the end of the runway. Left again, along a rutted mud road, deeply puddled, with mosquitoes skimming the puddles, beside a fence bordering the runway. The fifteen-minute ride had brought us thirty yards from the place our jet's wheels had touched down.

More to the point, as we soon learned, it had brought us thirty yards from the place wheels would lift off at that moment when the pilot shouts "Rotate!" above the din, and mighty engines go to full power.

(We had noticed during this journey a large hotel set near our own lodgings, behind a stucco wall, the "Caravanserai," let's call it. A friend who had stayed there during a business convention later told me of his terror his first afternoon, having shed his New York clothes down to his boxers, standing in those thunderbags looking seaward from his ninth-floor picture window, seeing fly, right toward his window, a wide-body, sliding into its landing path. On approach, aviators say, "Pan Am heavy." No amount of time, my friend said, would delete from his mind's eye his first sight of a jumbo at eye-level, coming at the conversation pit of his suite, at *him*. Not that there weren't other experiences to share with me later, like his first dip in the pool, an announcement coming over the hotel's public-address system: "Please, peoples. We have many complaints about pee-pee and doo-doo in swimming pool. Please don't forget to sign up for tonight's barbecue and salad bar on the beach.") But I'm making Sint Maarten sound like Iwo Jima, Bataan. I'm not writing *Guadalcanal Diary;* mine is a story of a heart murmur during a tropical vacation.

That first late afternoon we had a few unpleasant surprises in our seaside condominium, nothing acute: low water pressure from the taps and high voltage from the refrigerator door (we learned to pry it open using a mop handle). Otherwise, subtracting huge, lurid oil paintings of black-and-Day-Glo swans, the lodgings were dandy: slide the front door and there, fifteen yards dead ahead, was the sea.

Our view across the bay was dominated by a rusted dredger moored offshore from a monumental and immoderate timesharing project, a mausoleum of doomed real-estate speculation, the Pyramids of our time and that place. The half-baked and half-finished concrete resort and casino had been erected on land called Billy Folly, and was named Pelican Resort. Pelican because pelicans fished our common water, flying in threes, throttling back to stall speed, diving in a wingsback free fall, gobbling the catch. We learned to watch this process hours at a whack. That's what a Caribbean vacation is for, in my book, to zone out, narrow the concentration to what is least my own business. To buy a breather.

The pelicans' swooning fall and frantic takeoff reminded us of the enterprise at our backs, as though we could possibly have forgotten. The din began before breakfast, and quit during dinner. It was a stunning racket. What you hear at an airport isn't a patch on that uproar, because at an airport you don't pass your time in the open air a few feet from the runway. The blast shook the condo, shook us. It was not a Caribbean noise.

There was also a suspicion, vaguely perceived as a slickness to the epidermis, of oil finely sprayed at each takeoff. This was not Coppertone. Afterburners would cut in at full power, and those three or four great GEs or Pratt & Whitneys would go pedal to the metal, and we would cover our ears, and a fine mist of jet fuel would settle in the planes' wake, skim-coating my expensively vacationing family. Call it a vapor trail if you prefer; I call it kerosene.

The folks next door were untroubled by this phenomenon. They hailed from Queens, within easy earshot of JFK, and the takeoffs and landings made them feel at home. Our condominiums appeared to my untrained judgment identical, two-bedroom "units," but there seemed no end to this neighboring family. Each morning, as with passengers piling from a circus car, the cry was still *"they come!"* As many as they were, so were they similar, one big happy family.

Big! Here in Rhode Island there was a restaurant of legend, Custy's, all-you-can-eat. A few years ago it changed management, and on his first Sunday the new owner saw an out-of-state charter bus swing into his parking lot. As the bus unloaded its freight, anxiety turned to horror: a banner stuck to the bus's side proclaimed its origin and mission: THE BUFFET BUSTERS OF NEW JERSEY! (Custy's is out of business.)

Our neighbors were buffet busters, and we were at first standoffish when they approached us to share Sint Maarten dining lore. They had in their generous company a dog; his collar named him Butch, and he wouldn't be stood off. He would come to the *terraza* of our unit to scratch his ass against a chaise longue while we watched the rusty dredger and listened to planes take off. Butch would curl up, a hint of a smile baring his canines, and languidly masturbate, until we left him to his self-absorption and took our piña coladas indoors, where the swans hung motelly.

It didn't take long to notice that our Buffet Busters were having better fun than we. They laughed, and when they weren't laughing they smiled, like Butch. They seemed to love one another (but less ardently than Butch loved himself). Every morning they took a group picture, one member of the dozen or so grams and moms and in-laws darting out of the great assembly to memorialize the rest. Even their sunburns seemed to amuse them, and these were *sunburns,* the kind to be got only by spending hours without moving, floating belly-down staring at sand through a fogged face mask, or lying belly-up staring at the sky.

While these good and happy people took their ease, I was about my business. To protect myself against the consequences of hypertension, I boiled my blood driving crowded potholed roads searching for a doctor to give me a prescription. Failing, I wandered from town to town to town (there are three: two French, one Dutch) to entreat pharmacists for drugs, and to be insulted by them. At length, sweating and shaking like an addict from my frustrated mission, I found a worldly French druggist, all shrugs and tropical sophistication, dressed like Bogey in *Casablanca,* a coffin nail dangling from his lower lip. He was willing to sell me anything that wasn't what I had been instructed to use. I settled on reserpine, from *Rauwolfia serpentina,* Indian snakeroot. Potent.

After looking for The Man, finally making my connection, shopping in a supermarket whose linoleum floor, slick with spilled daiquiri mix, gave me a tumble amusing to other shoppers, I paused at one of the island's thousand or so casinos to lose my folding money to the wheel and my coins to the slots. At "home," going for a Heineken to wash down my drugs, I forgot what I had urged those in my care to remember, and got a hundred-plus volts, and this caused me, more in anger than in sorrow, to sweep my prescription Vuarnets violently from my brow to the floor, where a lens broke. That was my second full day in Sint Maarten.

The following days we fended off the friendly approaches of the Buffet Busters and the amorous urgencies of Butch. We swam. Mostly we spent money. We spent at casinos, with workaday stupidity. We could as easily have blown a wad at Nice, or Baden-Baden, or in Venice; I'm not even saying the company would have been classier in Europe. But the Sint Maarten casino crowd was very Atlantic City, *muy* San Juan.

We spent money eating. I mean *money*. We hadn't flown to the Islands to eat. We'd eaten in the Islands. We knew about Island cuisine. We'd tried veal birds at Bequia, "rack of jambon au mustard" in Antigua. We wished to eat and run, snack, go the simple route. So it was pizza for four at a fast-food place in Philipsburg, $83. American dollars. Dinner in Marigot, the French port, $200, plus tip *(sans vin)*, not an unwholesome piece of local fish, *tres nouvelle*, teensy.

The most pleasing restaurant in town we were told but did not, alas, believe, is *at* the airport, soundproofed against the din. Instead we chose a place set at the far end of the runway, very *intime*, popular with return visitors (who could they be, and what could they be thinking?), called Mary's Boon. It has evident charms: old wicker, a macaw in a cage (or maybe it was a fish in a bowl), guests got up in natural fibers, a single menu served take-it-or-leave-it at long, communal tables, an "honor bar," which means guests pour their own drinks, whose num-

ber they are honorbound to report, and for which they are charged
several dollars apiece, which imposed, to be honest, a heavy burden on
my sense of honor.

We ate at Mary's Boon with friends who knew the owners. Let's say
the bill was $300. (We ate some shrimp was why.) When it came time
to pay, we asked—discreetly I thought, so the other guests didn't have
to see the ugly transaction—if we might pay $150 a couple. It was a
matter of American Express traveler's checks, you see, because credit
cards—nasty plastic things—were not . . . honored.

"I don't want to get into this," said the owner. "One bill, one person
pays."

"Well, it's quite simple," I said. "We aren't asking for a mathematical
computation, just that you take half in checks from me, half in checks
from my friend."

"Must I speak more slowly?" the owner said. "What you do to each
other with your 'traveler's checks' is quite your own business. I wish to
have three hundred dollars, and I wish it from *one* of you."

Cross my heart.

Two days later, Christmas, my wife and I stopped for a couple of
drinks at La Samana ("untypical," the brochure says, "uncompro-
mised") where movie stars stay, but weren't staying that day. Our check
was $16. I offered a $50 traveler's check.

"Haven't you got something smaller?" asked the waitress at the least
compromised al fresco resort in the Caribbean, $520 a night double,
no meals, plus service.

But I run before my story. Back to Mary's Boon, or the hours following our honestly drunk drinks and $6-per-shrimp seafood at the
runway's end, so completely paid for. Sometime that night someone
broke into our unit, patrolled our bedroom while we slept, and stole
what was worth stealing, and much that was not. Now we were deep in
it: no keys, identification, credit cards, cash, or traveler's checks.

The Buffet Busters, worldly old hands, were resigned to our bad luck.

"See the plywood screwed over our slider?" (Indeed, we had remarked to ourselves the oddness of this use of a sliding-glass door fronting the ocean.) "Only thing to keep the fuckers out. And I keep a loaded hogleg on the night table."

But of course! How silly of us not to have thought of it.

"They come in boats. Swim ashore, grab the loot, they're gone. Did they get your medication?" (My medical adventures were not unknown to our immediate community: the single phone nearby worked according to the volume put into it, like a tin can connected to a tin can by string.) "They love drugs. One drug looks like another to those fellows."

We were told how lucky we were it was Christmas Eve morn; another day, and the Island would be shut tight till after New Year's. Many a red-letter day in the Lesser Antilles.

Karl Malden was on the money. We had the providence of having had stolen from us not just any traveler's checks but the right kind, and sure enough, American Express has a Philipsburg office, and I found my way to it. I stood in line to tell my grim tale, behind half a dozen or so other desolates, similarly deprived at poolside, on the beach, asleep in their hotels. I asked an agency employee if it was always like this, and was told, runically, that where there are casinos, tourists lose money.

Perhaps experience had educated the traveler's-check-refund people in their brisk manner, their refusal to say, as I might have liked to have heard: *This is tragic. Let us sit upon the ground and tell sad stories of the theft of cash.*

Or, at least: *Gee, downer, you must be bummed.*

Let *me* say it: I felt awful. Angry, hot, panicked. (I saw for the first time the glimmer of an improbable possibility: that a fellow might come to this island, get picked clean and never leave; such a fellow would wind down drinking Jamaican Red Cap beer, wearing white clothes that weren't white anymore and not caring that they weren't.)

I was also short of breath, as though a barber were wrapping a steaming towel around my face. I had felt this several times the past few days, and mentioned it to Priscilla, who took it more seriously than I took it. I wrote it off to heat, and stress, all those double saw-bucks flying pell-mell from my pockets into the pockets of strangers.

When I at last got to the head of the line of wronged ones, I learned that American Express would have no business with me until I filed a police report, which a policeman must sign. The American Express agent looked meaningfully at her watch, and explained that I had wasted much time in line, and the office closed, for Christmas and other holidays, in two hours, and I had better move with dispatch to the office of detectives, at the other end of Philipsburg's main drag.

Oh my! A speedy walk past the duty-free boom boxes and porcelain kitty-cats to another long line. As this crept, winding indoors from the hot alley where we miserables stood gnawing our lower lips, it dawned on me that to get a signature on a piece of paper was not so casually done as demanded.

"We hab no crime on dis island," I heard a detective explain. "Mainland peoples bring de trouble. And Dominicans." (As Turks are to Swiss, and Koreans to Japanese, the people of Dominica, who labor with their hands, are to the entrepreneurs of Sint Maarten. It is a time-worn story.)

Lacking criminals, the detectives made do with victims. The victim immediately ahead of me was an Islander. His story was sadder and more complicated than mine. It seems that the night before, a person or persons unknown had invaded his property, taking advantage of the peculiarity that it was without a cyclone fence ringed with razor wire, and made away with the man's dog. The detective stopped writing, and looked up. The dog could be identified, the victim explained, and began to give an account of an animal I could have sworn was our neighbor Butch, until I heard a final detail: "My dog got three legs." (Butch had five, always.)

My interview was not successful. The detective, studying my lack of composure, the red-faced urgency of my manner, concluded that I was a confidence man, and he was no stranger to "devices" as he assured me. We were soon on the subject of signatures. I wanted his, in any form, on anything. I had an easier time getting the Splendid Splinter's when I was a boy. I believed I might weep. The detective saw something in me that made him wish I would go away, as the former master of a three-legged dog had gone away, and I explained that I *would* go away, but only with a detective's signature. And that is how I got a name written on my airline ticket, which the cat burglar(s) had neglected to steal. This signature I rushed to the outskirts of Philipsburg, a town composed of outskirts, to a Dutch bank. Here, American Express had sort of suggested, the detective's signature would be exchanged for traveler's checks. Waiting in line, I was offered a fruit punch—rum-and-cherry Slurpee, with a custard garnish. These were served by a Dutch bank officer who was busy drinking most of those portions of the concoction she was pouring for her puzzled customers; I thought I saw a pathway to her sympathy if not her heart, and invited her to enjoy the cup she extended toward me. In turn she invited me to sit at her desk. Her fingernails were too long to make it possible for her to open ledgers, but she invited me to her cabin after the close of business to "happify Yuletime." I promised that that cabin was the only place I longed to be, and got new traveler's checks, and the residue of her lurid lipstick on my nose. (She had removed her bifocals to cuddle me.)

The rest of our holiday was less fun.

Well, let me be fair. Putting aside an episode with our rented automobile in Marigot—where it was sideswiped while parked and while we ate a hundred dollars' worth of sandwiches on Christmas night, a mischance that would cost me two (maybe three) hundred, and resulted in a fight so terrible between Priscilla (who parked the car) and her husband (who signed the rental contract that left us nakedly exposed to the driving skills and honor of other people) that my children preferred to hike to their runway-side villa, from France to Holland, by shank's mare so they wouldn't be obliged to listen to a Mr. & Mrs. that ended only because I ran out of breath to prolong it—Christmas was mezzo-mezzo.

During our holiday disagreement, I asked speculatively: "Will we ever get off this miserable island?"

The next day I found a way.

For a consideration a catamaran, the *Bluebeard*, chartered on a head-boat basis (charging per passenger to all comers), would sail us from Marigot to Sandy Island, a reef-girt sandspit two hundred by fifty yards, a couple of miles northwest of Anguilla. Anguilla, under British colonial rule, is the place to which people flee when the pressure of Sint Maarten screws too tight on them; Sandy Island is where they go when the bustle of Anguilla mills them down.

The arrangements were businesslike. In the shadow of a casino I bought three tickets (Priscilla was left to guard the few remaining dollars and, especially, the plane tickets), and we were to surrender these dockside next day to the crew of *Bluebeard*. We were up early; I felt hinky, wanted to leave time aplenty for the untoward to waylay us before boarding. I believed two hours would be adequate for the seven-mile journey to Marigot by sideswiped car, time enough surely to find a bulletproof parking place. I wanted this to go smoothly.

It did not; we were rained out.

We took it well. Yachtsmen we were, sports. There was always to-morrow, our last full day. And tomorrow, in fact, came without in-tervening tragedy. We never left home, and remembered to open the refrigerator with a long wooden stick, and took baths instead of show-ers, so we wouldn't fall down and injure ourselves, and kept our doors and windows shut and locked, all day, even after the rain stopped, so our tickets and passports would not be stolen by foreigners who come from the sea. No pelicans fell on us while we swam.

Come next morning, I got Nicholas and Justin up with the sun, and packed, and found we were just that little bit short of suntan lotion. We stopped at a convenience store along the imperfectly executed "road" to Marigot, and bought Sea & Ski, for only fifteen dollars. I rummaged for the money at the bottom of a canvas bag holding our *Bluebeard* tickets. I had examined these tickets several times that morning, had held them in my hands, had stared at them and read their promises: the bracing sail, the "dazzling white beach, the coral reefs that teem with bright, colorful tropical fish set in incredibly blue waters." I had not failed to note that after "complimentary beverages" the "magical sound of a conch horn announces the readiness of a plentiful barbe-cue" on the beach.

So: we parked the sideswiped vehicle in Marigot and walked briskly toward the yacht basin, and then—half an hour before we were to sail—I felt an inkling that we and our tickets were no longer together. A cursory look in my canvas bag revealed this horribly to be so. Throwing the bag to a son, yelling over my shoulder "Beg them to wait" I ran to the car, and drove it, in violation of sense and law, ca-reening around curves, ignoring a red light at a drawbridge, *fast,* to the "convenience" store. Breathless I broke in ahead of other customers.

"I left my tickets."

"What you talking about?"

"Hey, we were in line."

"Tickets. Suntan lotion. Counter."

And then it dawned on me. To black people, white people look alike. I am bald, and wear a white beard, and stutter, but the woman who twenty minutes earlier had instructed me to have a nice day did not know me. I tell you: it hurt.

"Could my tickets be in your wastebasket?"

And then I was behind the counter, rummaging through trash, while her husband or co-worker or brother or son or father came toward me with a look that would have frightened me had I had the composure to feel fear.

"You stole our tickets," I reasoned. "I will never shop here again," I promised. "Fifteen dollars for Sea & Ski is not right. I will tell about this. I am," I explained, "a *writer!*"

And then I drove back to Marigot, weeping. There would be for us no "magical sound of a conch horn," no "plentiful barbecue." I may weep again, maybe ten minutes from now. But I had not wept for many years until then, and have not wept since, and while I wept, I drove as recklessly as a teenager, with the difference that by then I knew as I had not known when I was sixteen that I could die, or kill, driving like that.

Parked and ran, and again found it difficult to breathe, but now there was an iron band under my arms cinching my chest.

The boat was preparing to sail.

"She stole the tickets."

"Chill out," Nicholas said.

"Take it easy," a crew member suggested. "Have you looked in your pockets? Checked that ice bag?"

"Of course I have!" Now I was yelling, while Justin dug his hands deep into the bag and found, where I had put them for safekeeping, the tickets.

It was as promised. Free drinks, sunshine, cool breezes, grilled fish. I apologized to everyone, blushing, my heart pounding with shame, I thought. The passengers were not boors. The crew were not cynical beach bums. They forgave me. I put aside a twenty-dollar bill to tip them generously for the trouble I had put them to. I wanted them to know I was not as I seemed. I began to relax. I could be a good guy. Tomorrow we'd be gone. My tip would go far to set things right. As we approached Marigot at day's end, I lay on deck, rolled to my left, and watched a twenty-dollar bill, the only money any Wolff had aboard, blow from my pocket, and bob in our wake. Justin saw it all, and looked away:

"Wow," he said.

Our flight was to leave at four. We had been forewarned of chaos at the airport, long lines at the ticket counter, passport control, customs. We agreed to arrive at two. We packed. At noon my wife prepared to take a shower. My sons and I decided on a final swim. In the sea, for a reason I cannot fathom, I decided I wanted a water-fight; I wanted the kind of water-fight *they* fight once a year, the real McCoy, not just splashing, but dunking, wrestling, slick violence. Me versus them. They played horse, and wrestled me down, and I remember my head going under, and coming up trying to catch a breath, and not getting a full load in my lungs, and then running toward them in deeper water, my legs heavy against the surge, feeling not right, turning toward shore, walking deliberately toward a beach chair set at the sea's edge, understanding that to reach that chair not thirty feet away would be to get somewhere I *had* to reach, not as though my life depended on reaching that aluminum-and-plastic chaise longue, but as though it were an important goal, in the sense that one might run to board a slow-moving train that was not the last train ever to roll to one's destination, but what the hell, one had not come so far to miss trains.

I got there, sort of. I was trying hard to breathe. I managed to say to my older son, "I can't breathe."

But I couldn't find the posture to inhale what I wanted so badly. Upright, dignified: not enough air, something pinched off. Slump-shouldered, sagging: the diaphragm wouldn't deliver.

I tried to lie down.

"Lower this chair for me, Nick."

What happened then I didn't witness. As far as I know, I asked my son a favor, and the next thing, just a blink out of my life, there were people standing above me, and I heard a little girl crying, and asking, "Is he dead?"

What bad manners, I remember thinking. Much later I was told that was no little girl, but my wife. I had no trouble recognizing the voices of my sons, who were saying, not in unison but at the same time, two incantations, a fugue: "Be all right. Don't give up. Come back." And much else.

It was embarrassing, all those strangers.

A Buffet Buster was holding my wrist. "He's got a pulse again."

She knew her apples.

I tried to reassure them. I wanted to walk away from all this, and even then I knew it was important to escape that island. I didn't try to stand, but when I spoke I made my voice purposeful: "I'm okay."

No one seemed interested in my opinion of myself, because they had seen what I hadn't: gray skin, eyes rolled back under my lids, convulsions—to the untrained eyes of my wife and sons, death.

Now—soon—came a doctor, Dutch, running. I mistook him for a jogger.

Then the ambulance, a wild ride to Philipsburg, just wild; what a trip, lying on my back below the scream of the siren and seeing, blurred beyond the distracted nurse, palm trees shoot by.

"Where are my glasses?"

"Just calm down, Dad. We'll be there. Please be quiet. Don't worry."

But, my God, Nicholas was edgy, the laid-back one, a grace-under-pressure boy. What was going on? I was, as they say, beside myself, trying without success to share a secret: *I was okay.*

The Dutch physician from the beach was met at the emergency room by a Dutch cardiologist, and they laid me down and hooked me up and asked questions. Was I in pain? (No.) Where had the pain come? Shoulders? Arms?

Now this called for a more complicated reply than seems invited by such simple questions. My situation with the doctors was a bit like the situation of someone guessing which hand holds a coin. If the tempting obvious guess is *right hand,* a simpleminded guesser will say *left,* a more subtle mind *right,* subtler still *left.* . . . I knew what story was told by pain radiating from the shoulders, and the doctors guessed I knew this and would deny it, and I denied it because I had not felt it, but the doctors had to decide whether I denied it because I had not felt it or because I didn't want to have had a heart attack.

The vocabulary of pain is discriminating. I aimed to illuminate rather than disguise my difficulty, but the emergency room of a Caribbean hospital is not precisely the site of choice for precise lexical delicacy. A patient's diction can express, and it can delude. Words, we do not tire of reminding ourselves, count. There is "sharp," "dull," "throbbing," "hot," "unbearable," "steady." I had experienced none of these sensations; instead, hurried, I chose an approximate locution, inaccurate in fact, but in the spirit of my experience: "It felt like a heavy person kneeling on my chest."

Oh, how vigorously I would later try to retract those words, to delete them from my transcript, to change my grade. But they were my

words, and I said them close to the moment, and they went from English to Dutch back out to English, and they added up to the single
conclusion I least believed or wanted to believe: *heart attack.*

Now the EKG. I lay in the emergency room, watching the terror on
Priscilla's face and Justin's; I couldn't imagine what they were thinking.
My attention was in the present tense; now a nurse was exclaiming im-
patiently that the monitor cups wouldn't adhere to my white-haired
chest; now she was shaving my chest; now I felt the cold shock of jelly
rubbed on me to hold the cups. I listened to doctors discuss, in a language I could not have understood had it been English, what it was
with me. I knew I was just fine, that once this rigmarole was finished,
I'd fly home and put paid to this fiasco of a holiday.

The diagnosis was heart disease. Syncopes here and abnormal repolar-
izations there. I tried to argue them out of it, explaining that I had been
using reserpine, a drug new to me. That must have keeled me over, the
reserpine. My instinctive distrust of that drug was not, I later learned,
as desperately farfetched as you might believe. Reserpine is potent, can
provoke suicidal depressions that hang on for months. More to my
point, it so slows the heartbeat as sometimes to cause fainting, not to
mention rashes, weight increase, lethargy, troubled dreams, blurred
vision, nosebleeds, premature ejaculation: let's conclude that depression is a side effect of these side effects.

I explained about my medications: they were in my driveway, all
could be traced to that ill beginning. The Dutch doctors were curious
as to how I managed to prescribe for myself a drug so potent as reserpine, and I mentioned Marigot, a pharmacy there, and they looked at
each other, illuminated.

"Ah, the French." The doctors shrugged, so predictably that I
laughed! But I found myself laughing alone.

It was decided, without interest in my opinion, that I would be checked into the hospital and observed until more was known. The stethoscope, the charts, did not suggest the side effects of reserpine.

I gave in. Tame as a puppy. Fact was, I wanted to be in a room alone, with the door shut. I was done now searching for better words, wondering *what next*, reckoning how we would escape that botched island. I wanted to nap.

I was wheeled into an air-conditioned room, with a window fronting the harbor. I was getting my hand held by one and then another of my family, and that was nice, but—I thought—theatrical, uncustomary. More familiar was the nature of Priscilla's question to my sons after I was hooked up to a monitor by wires leading from my breasts, ankles; the monitor, just like the television monitors you've seen (I mean the ones *on* television, *St. Elsewhere*, say), clicked busily but irregularly, sketched peaks and valleys, jagged yellow lines.

My wife asked my boys, the cardiologists: "Does that look right to you? It doesn't look right to me."

And then they left me to rest.

Immediately came a nutritionist, asking was I hungry; I said no, not a bit hungry. So she produced for me to eat—half an hour after the emergency room, an hour beyond the ambulance, an hour and fifteen minutes after the water fight—chicken creole. There were French fries, and butterscotch pudding, and a huge breast of chicken with tomato sauce and okra. There were thick slabs of white bread. A bottle of Orange Crush. If I had asked for a St. Pauli Girl, I could have had it, and a squash racquet too. When the food was removed, I thought I might rest.

I remembered a story a friend told me about his adventure in Jamaica thirty years ago during spring vacation from boarding school. Shy around girls, he was quite a diver, so he had put in hour upon hour diving from cliffs to amaze them but was then unable to hear their amazement. Water had collected in his ears, and he did what we do: shook his head violently, jumped on the left foot, jumped on the right, whacked the sides of his head with his palms. He bought Jamaican Q-tips, cotton swabs just the wrong size, and they seemed to drive the water deeper in his ears and to cause some small pain.

His roommate knew a remedy, was surprised it was not a remedy familiar to all divers: "Pour bourbon in your ears. Melts the wax, and flushes out the salt water."

In Jamaica, thirty years ago, bourbon was scarce, but there was 151-proof rum, and my friend poured this in one ear and then, despite the sensation you may guess at, poured some in the other ear. He spent time in a Caribbean hospital. The hospital stay made an impression on him—changed him even.

"Do you believe in Our Lord Jesus *Christ!*"

She was immense, a figure only Flannery O'Connor could have imagined, breasts like shoats squirming to escape from a croaker sack. Black she wore, and a florid hat, and plum lipstick. Rouged, bearing a Bible.

"I say, do you *believe* in Him!"

For a moment, I almost thought of thinking whether I believed in anything the way she needed to know whether I believed in Him. Instead I thought, I don't need this.

"No."

"I say, will you *declare* your belief in the Son of God!"

"Please go away."

She was astounded. She was rattling off a rap from memory, let's call it a litany. This was not in the script, getting shown the door, on *Sunday*.

"I do this by the commandment of the Lord Jesus Christ! This is my day off work."

"Take a load off," I said. "Enjoy a day of rest. I'm a bad customer."

"I'll tell you, mister, you are sick! They told me."

"Go away."

The apostle dropped to her knees. Her hat was ornate, almost interesting.

"There ain't no hospital beds in Hell, mister. Pray with me!"

I rolled over, away from the missionary's hat, and looked out at the harbor. A cruise ship was coming in. My eyes without my glasses saw it all blurred. I was infirm, unwell. But I could hear the clanking anchor chain and a bustle below my window on the beach, the excitement of people near a place where money will soon be redistributed. I never heard the proselyte leave, but I knew she was gone, and with her the Good News.

Later that night, Priscilla came back with the boys. Justin thought it might be interesting to touch together the two electric paddles, those things you see in television emergency rooms, when the intern yells "clear!" and gives some luckless sod the juice, and the patient's chest heaves, and his legs buck like a bronc's, and his monitor line goes wavy ("We've got a pulse; his blood pressure's coming back!") and everyone smiles, or it goes flat ("I need a drink. Sometimes I hate this job! Anyone coming?"). Anyway, Justin was bringing the resurrection paddles together, Priscilla yelled at him, I jerked, my own life-sign line went kind of jagged, and Priscilla and I argued. Was what I might have had on the beach properly called a "myocardial infarction" (my choice), or "myocardial infraction" (Priscilla's and, once they heard the two side by side, the boys' choice). I was right, but let's concede "infraction" makes a world more sense.

Then Priscilla, just before they left me for the night, said, "I'll never be mean to you again."

She meant it too. It made me laugh.

"Don't say such a thing. It makes me sad to hear it. I can't do without."

"I mean it. I'll never be mean to you again."

Well.

Near midnight, finished with a junk novel I was reading to keep my mind off my worries, which were worrying me less than they should, I got to my window, stretching to their farthest reach the wires connecting me to the heart monitor. I was drawn by lights in the harbor, and friendly shouts from the beach. I leaned my nose against the pane and tried to focus. Below on the beach I could see what looked like fireflies, wavy flickers seeming to signal to the sparkling cruise ship offshore, dressed with lights; to my blear vision the vessel seemed afire. My attention was drawn to a noise below, and I realized what I must seem to anyone looking in my window, an old geezer with cups stuck to his tits, wires leading out. The fireflies came closer, and I thought someone was waving sparklers at me in a friendly way, and then I saw the orange trail of a comet arc toward me, and then felt an awful concussion, full explosion, and I heard glass break, and by the time the nurses were there, in response to that monitor honking like a French flic's car, I realized someone had lobbed a cherry bomb at me, and the outer of the two windows had been shattered by it.

So I lay awake waiting for the blood test whose results would tell me whether I had had a myocardial in*far*ction, killing a region of my heart, or whether something else had made me eat sand. I lay tense, looking toward the open door where the evangelist in black might appear again with her Holy Book and Glad Tidings, and then toward the window, waiting for another bang. Staring out the window, I saw the nimbus of the sun rise and had blood drawn, and heard a doctor tell me the blood test revealed none of those enzymes that accompany a death of heart muscle; I had probably not had the experience called heart attack.

"How soon can I get off this dangerous island?"

"Next week, five or six days, after we observe you."

"Today," I said.

I was warned not on any account to show signs of malaise at the airport, or the airlines would never carry me off that unspeakable place for fear I'd make trouble for them: die, say, or—worse—litigate them. It was an odd sensation, but not at all unpleasant, to be coddled by my family, to have my bags toted by Justin while Nicholas checked us in, to have Priscilla deal with the wrecked rent-a-car, and gesticulate, and argue, and by sweet advocacy save a buck or two. (I would have fought to win a moral judgment, which is one reason, I guess, I have high blood pressure. Priscilla just wanted to get the damage payment down a little, bless her.)

In fact, I felt fine, okay, not so bad. Tired, distracted, but I managed to watch the sappy holiday movie, a colorized *It's a Wonderful Life*. I began to notice, as Jimmy Stewart finally noticed, the decencies manifest around me. Flying north, into the teeth of a winter whose forthright sharpness I welcomed, I thought how kind the Buffet Busters had been, how quick to help, how competent. Even Butch, watching me heave back to life on my beach chaise, cocked his head, concerned more about me, it seemed, than about his pecker. I didn't like the news the Dutch doctors gave me, but they gave it, on a Sunday. The appraiser at the car rental—LUCKY (!) CAR RENTALS—had been just. As our stay at the condo was necessarily lengthened, instead of bills we got checks, refunds to atone for the nastiness of the refrigerator; the extra night was on them, they insisted cheerfully.

I was learning lessons. Not the kind that is taught with a club that knocks you down: that kind of lesson I had always expected to have forced on me, and in fact it taught me nothing, except to remind me, around my family, of something Priscilla had read, that the one thing nobody says on his deathbed is "I wish I'd worked harder."

I was looking ahead to complicated news, though on New Year's Day I didn't guess how complicated. The messages coming in were about ratio, proportion; everywhere I turned people tried to smooth things for me. Near-strangers would write. Friends with whom I had nursed antique grievances—feuds blossoming black from disputes over how many portholes in a 1951 Buick Special, or why didn't you like my book better, or pick up that dinner check, or phone earlier when you knew you couldn't come for the weekend, or help with the dishes when you came? These people were kind, wise, on call.

Snow fell with us on Kennedy. In the customs shed the boys fought for luggage, and Priscilla tried to learn whether Providence was snowed in, whether flights would leave for that place, whether the parking lot there had been plowed. I telephoned doctors. I telephoned my father-in-law, a surgeon. For many years he had wisely dismissed as beneath serious discussion his family's anxious questions about sore throats and aching feet. To this story he listened. His interest did not reassure me. Neither did the product of a late-night conversation with my new doctor. He wanted me in his office tomorrow, no kidding.

I got a crash course in cardiology. While I was keeling over in Sint Maarten, my doctor at home had been studying pictures and numbers from that echocardiogram administered three years earlier; these had not shown him "the heart of a baby"; these had sufficiently alarmed him that he was telephoning our house while I was snorkeling off the *Bluebeard,* losing money at roulette, all the rest. He was not surprised, alas, by what I told him, and brought forth cutaway pictures of the heart and especially of the heart's valves, and especially of the aortic region.

Priscilla and Nicholas sat through his patient explanation. I had found books about prescription drugs, and had photocopied—let's say obsessively—the dire, possible (improbable) side effects of reserpine. Surely this explained everything. A reflex had evolved: at the end of every test I expected to hear: *Go home, you silly goose! There's nothing wrong with you. Reserpine tossed you a curve ball is all.*

The doctor listened. The doctor said, "Anything's possible." The doctor got me an emergency appointment with a cardiologist.

The cardiologist was laconic, self-assured. He resembled Hal Holbrook, and gave off that same aura of prematurely gray-haired competence. This was not the man on whom I wished to exercise my reserpine theory of fainting. The cardiologist didn't at first seem to have, as Priscilla put it, "a heart as big, as all outdoors." (We were compiling an omnium-gatherum of clichés; I didn't resist the temptation to call friends on their expressions: "You'd die to see her," "My heart's with you," "I feel heartsick for you"; my favorite, after a chest X-ray revealed my abnormally enlarged pump—"You're all heart.")

The cardiologist listened, and listened harder where other doctors had listened hard, and listened there some more. He was brisk; his hands were delicate; as he finished with me, he patted me on the head. I could have wept with gratitude for that gentle touch; Priscilla, watching, said it was like a man patting a dog. She was right; I was right. The pat was perhaps condescending, but if ever I wanted to be touched from above, from Olympus by a god, it was that day. I didn't want a cardiologist who was my equal; I knew what I was and was not. I knew how inaccurately I could parse a paragraph, or misdiagnose a meaning. I wanted to be in the hands of a master.

This master didn't like to answer questions. He especially winced at *what-if* questions; they made him less terse than silent as a tomb. He knew what he knew, would tell when it came time to tell. He knew what he *thought.* He thought I had acute aortic valvular stenosis, which meant my aortic valve was defective, narrow, failing properly to open, which meant I was not pumping sufficient oxygen-rich blood up my ascending aorta, the great artery, to my body—to my brain, for example. (Thus one faints, falls down, and the head—if all goes according to the inventor's plan—lies below the heart, and is fed by gravity.) But I learned what aortic valvular stenosis meant from *The Book of Knowledge* later. In that office then, I learned only that the cardiologist wanted me to get a chest X-ray and have another echocardiogram, immediately. I had been warned that I might have to undergo a procedure called "cardiac catheterization," which I loosely understood to be the threading of a long tube up an artery and into the heart, where pressures could be read, and dye injected and photographed as it snaked through tributaries.

An echocardiogram, by high contrast, is performed in Rhode Island Hospital's cardiac "non-invasive" wing. Oh, I liked "non-invasive." Give me "non-invasive" any day. It uses Doppler, a radar that can translate sound waves into pictures and numbers. The snowy Saturday morning Nicholas drove me to the hospital to have my heart televised, we found in the waiting room an aged couple. It was no trick to know which of them was there to be tested: her face was gray, and she trembled from stone terror. Later, I would think that to have seen her was to look into a mirror, but now it seemed I was on one side of a high fence, and she on the other.

Nicholas talked to her. The weather. The Patriots. How 'bout those Celtics! His college courses and summer jobs. Smart boy: she was forgetting here and now; forgetting herself, almost. This was life, talking this way.

"Does it hurt?" her husband asked me.

I wondered whether he thought I was a doctor. I wondered what they had been told, whether they too had thumbed an encyclopedia. I thought how needless *this* terror was.

"Not a bit."

In fact it did hurt, a bit. Not me, as it turned out, but the nurse who made her way by microphones up and down and across me. The examining room, all electronics and monitors, was dark, so only the green light of the monitor lit us dimly, as murky pale as the floor of a shoal sea.

I heard the murmur, a surfy snuffle, a wet whisper, like this: *be at peace, be at peace, be at peace.* Say it fast, honest. That's what my heart, amplified and sounded, said.

The nurse working me over was teaching the procedure to a nurse from another hospital. The student was bored and distracted; she chewed gum loudly enough to have the noise picked up by the echocardiogram mike, and was asked to give her jaws a rest.

"Where do you get these handiwipes?" she asked her teacher. "I love these; they're pre-moistened. I wish I had some at home," she said. "They sure are handy."

My nurse was annoyed. She wasn't seeing the pictures she was told to shoot.

"Aortic stenosis has terrible mike angles. It kills, really hurts my hand to have to hold the mike this way. What a hassle."

"For me, too," I said.

"Quiet," she said, but the gum-chewer didn't obey.

"One thing for sure," I had told Priscilla that morning. "No one, *no way,* is threading anything up my arteries into my heart. Go to the bank on it."

In fact, walking a short distance from a Newport parking lot to my bank, less than two blocks, I had felt a catch in my lungs, a want of something. Breathe as I would, I couldn't get a full shot. (I popped a nitroglycerine tablet under my tongue, the time-honored remedy for victims of angina, but because angina wasn't my problem, the "nitro"—as it's known to its friends—was no remedy.) Two days later, two weeks after my felling in the Islands, I tried to drag a garbage can fifteen yards up my driveway, and I couldn't. I stood in the cold that day, alone in the small town where we live, and put a hand under my jacket and under my shirt, and tried to feel my heart, as though it were willing to tell me what it wanted, what I had done to it.

As soon as the chest X-ray was in the cardiologist's hands (confirming that my heart was abnormally enlarged, from laboring to pump blood through a bum valve), together with the echocardiogram, I was told the next step was to thread a wire up my arteries into my heart.

"How soon?" I asked.

"Beginning of next week," he said.

My cardiologist would not discuss what lay beyond cardiac catheterization, which would confirm his suspicions, or—lots of luck—confound them. I knew. The encyclopedia explained it all under Cardiac Abnormalities. Next they "crack your chest," and the knife goes to work.

But, for now, we weren't to discuss sharp knives. Our topic was catheterization. This we discussed in the cardiologist's office, examining a model of a heart, organs cleverly fit within organs, a contraption of hinges and lurid colors. I watched him manipulate it, and pretended to understand what I was being told, much of it in Latin.

But about the procedure he couldn't have been clearer. He told me everything, because this was not speculative; this would happen. He explained hospital admission, and what and when I would eat, and when I would begin my fast, and when and where they would wheel me down to the catheterization ("Cardiac Intensive Unit" presumably) room, and what would run through my IV, tranquilizing me, and who would do what, and for how long, and what I would feel.

"It will hurt when you get the local anesthesia. We'll give you a shot right next to the groin. Then the pain will dull. We'll insinuate a tube up your femoral artery; it is about the diameter of linguini; no nerves there, so it won't hurt. Then we'll thread another into your coronary arteries, to look into heart disease." (Blocked coronary arteries; insufficient blood *to* the heart; bypass country.)

Before I could ask, he told me: "we have problems a few times for a hundred procedures. These can vary: heart attack, stroke. It is possible to puncture a vital artery."

My cardiologist is known both vulgarly and respectfully as a "cath jockey." If there was anyone in the neighborhood I was prepared to trust with wires the size of pasta, and with my vital stuff, there he sat. He smiled; I melted with gratitude.

What he said would happen happened. It was an operating room, with a jungle of wires and screens. Many technicians, two cardiologists. The IVs had been run into me, thinning my blood, or thickening it, tranquilizing me. I got the shot, and never felt the deep incision about two inches from the jewel box (my jewel box), where they cut into the artery. I felt pressure. I was awake, and was to remain awake, eyes wide open, so I could issue reports, and "cooperate," holding my breath, exhaling.

Meantime, the team talked. They were all business, looking, judging what they saw. A time came when I knew the wire was at my aortic valve (such as it was), because they told me, and because I felt something I didn't like, a crazy quickening of the beat. This called for a shot, right into an open vein, and mechanisms calmed again, and I heard the subtlest change of pitch and attention in the cardiologist's running commentary into a tape recorder. I had been all smiles, believed I was getting a good report card. Then someone whistled and said, *"That's tight!"*

That was the valve.

Then they warned me they were about to inject dye, to get pictures, an angiogram, to see whether my coronary arteries were silted with fat, whether maybe they needed to be bypassed with a length of vein from my leg, *my* leg.

I had been warned the dye ("contrast medium") would give discomfort, a few-second hot shot through my body. Precisely as foretold: discomfort rather than pain, and great heat, which soon passed.

"Let's get the stuff out now."

And bingo, after an hour's work, about noon, they were done with looking.

In the hall outside, while they did another customer inside (we were parked like cars on a full lot), an intern leaned for twenty minutes with his full weight on my groin's bleeding artery. He explained I'd have a sandbag on it the following twenty-four hours, and if there were no complications, I could go home tomorrow.

My cardiologist told me I'd be thirsty when it was over. I'd fasted twelve hours—neither food nor water—so the dye could do its thing without making me puke, and the dry surgical theater . . . I was thirsty. And just as my cardiologist had promised in his office last week, he appeared with a root-beer popsicle. I hadn't eaten a root-beer twin-stick popsicle since I was a kid. Had they been out there all this time? Oh boy! It was sweet, and on the instant I was hooked.

"Where do you get these?" I asked.

The cardiologist looked at me as though he had something else on his mind. Why so closemouthed? Why not share his connection? Who needed him: if Chasen's flew chili to Rome during the filming of *Cleopatra,* I could get root-beer popsicles sent to Rhode Island.

Not twenty-four hours earlier I had told Priscilla: "One thing for *damned sure.* No way, José, are they 'cracking' this chest." I had banged my breast for emphasis. "I'll go to the dye and linguini, but beyond the pasta, count me out." I knew a thing or two myself: how a local cardiologist, Dr. Belasco, had got himself in the steel chateau the year before for putting pacemakers in people whose hearts needed no pacing. I had just seen a report on *20/20* about the failure of mechanical mitral valves, with consequences you don't want even to imagine, and you haven't got one in you. And I had read a letter to the *New York Times* on the subject of heroic rescue of heart-diseased patients, from a Florida woman who wanted next time her heart played tricks on her to wake up dead. Called "Don't Save Me Again," the letter said, in part:

I had open-heart surgery after two years in bed with congestive heart failure. I was a pioneer in valve replacement. This was followed by hepatitis (bad blood transfusion), coronary (valvular clot), hysterectomy (bleeding from anticoagulants), loss of vision (cerebrovascular accident), loss of ability to read (stroke), open-heart surgery (replacement of first mitral valve), more open-heart surgery (bleeding in chest cavity), cranial and internal bleeding (anticoagulants).

Call me a stubborn fool, but I thought I'd take a pass on the chest cracking.

The cardiologist spoke: "Your aortic valve is badly stenosed."

"A mess?"

He nodded.

"How soon can we get someone to cut it out?"

It was a genetic botch. It would be tidy to believe that the defect was a patrimony, given my persistent labors to memorialize in written and oral history my father's peculiar legacy to his sons. I had thought that his estate—twenty-five dollars—shared equally with my brother, was the last of him.

Save for memories, it was. If my poor excuse for an aortic valve can be blamed on either parent's genes, I'd have to choose my mother's; her own unlucky mother died at forty-one of mitral stenosis and re- gurgitation, the failure of the other principal heart valve. In fact, even that sad end probably had nothing to do with my state, inasmuch as my grandmother was known to have had rheumatic fever, a common cause of heart-valve disorders.

No, this was no one's fault. Not my father's, not my mother's, not even mine. The *"why me?"* mechanism never kicked in. It made all the sense in the world that my aortic valve was stupid. It was just a thing that happens sometimes to some people. The night before my op- eration, the surgeon was very clear about things. To have my chest sawed and cut open, to be put on a heart-lung machine, to cut into the aorta to remove something, and replace it with something else— man-made—this was not without risks.

Maybe five of a hundred patients don't come out of the operating room alive. Improving these pretty good odds were my otherwise good health, his celebrated skill, his faith in the valve he meant to sew in me. He was serene, a late-night reader, *very* late-night, after a day of scheduled heart surgery, followed by the unforeseen: shotgunned chests, ice-picked pumps. He was too busy for a bedside manner, but he admired good writing. I hoped he liked my prose. I thought if maybe he admired my writing, maybe I'd have an edge, maybe even get what a friend in a similar fix got from his heart surgeon, a written guarantee that my friend would *never* die. That kind of edge. On the other hand, maybe I'd do without the edge, and the cutting. What then, I asked the man who was next morning to hold my heart in his hands.

Oh, for sure, without a valve replacement, I could expect to live maybe another year, probably less than half that.

What was to decide?

The morning Nicholas drove me to the hospital, I sat at my desk in what an in-law had called our "Terminal House" (because it is commodious enough to store a lifetime collection of junk), paying bills working on—can you believe it?—taxes. Deposited (I know, I wouldn't believe it either) a "kill-fee" for a failed commissioned essay that was— as editors sometimes say—lifeless.

The night before the dawn cutting-in, considerate nurses and counselors said what they needed to say, clarified, explained, explained again. While they were "in," as they said, "there," they might do that bypass, but probably would not. Time, I was told, is precious on a heart-lung machine. I feigned comprehension.

Priscilla and Justin and Nicholas had come and gone and come and gone. They were great. Justin saved the occasion from sobersidedness. I mentioned that I needed bifocals.

"Dad," he said, "did it occur to you that you were twenty-what—thirty, maybe—when Nick was born . . ."

"Twenty-nine . . ."

"Twenty-nine. *Old.* Too late to have kids. Irresponsible. You can't even throw a ball to your tykes. Now from four-eyes to six-eyes. Lousy foresight."

To them, I had something that was bust, and could merely be fixed. I took peace from them. They wanted to see me as soon as it was over, in the intensive care unit, seemed to look forward to it, as to a happy ceremony. The surgeon had not exactly discouraged them, but I could tell, and Priscilla could tell, he'd sooner they waited. He suggested that I would make an alarming sight to people unused to seeing a person fresh from open-heart surgery. (Later, when I was thought well enough to be told such stories, I heard about a woman who came to see her husband—immediately post-op, as they say—minutes after a valve replacement. The shocking sight of him—his color, facial slackness, less man than junction box for wires and tubes—blew her heart, killed her dead.)

Alone, I willed myself to think *de profundis* about what was about to be done to me, to happen after. It has been a point of dispute between me and people I love that I suffer from a failure of gravity. I excuse myself by believing it wrong to confuse seriousness with solemnity, to pull a long face when I believe, believe right in my heart, that most things are funny. I do not exclude death, entirely. I know (but have had little experience) of deaths that were not appropriately funny, but I don't dishonor them with easy pieties.

My own imagination, for worse or better, inclines toward absurd ends. I was once in a near-collision at sea, aboard a famous Mediterranean steamship, flagship of the fleet, in the Straits of Gibraltar on a clear and moonlit night, when she altered course to draw close and salute her sister ship. It was a very close escape, and I knew in that moment that had it happened, my friends would learn of it and feel awful, but that part of the story, an important part, would be difficult to resist as comic narrative.

Or difficult for me. I'm sorry.

Now, though, I wasn't laughing. On the other hand, I wasn't frightened. (I put this down to consoling ignorance, but I also put it down to a temperamental abhorrence of theatricality.) What *would* have frightened me was root canal. I don't have any notion what root canal is, and I don't want to know.

Lying alone that night, I thought ruefully that I might miss by more than a little my ambition to check out debt-free and penniless. Let me just say that as difficult as it would have been for pals and kin to walk this planet without me, it would have been catastrophic for Visa and Diners' Club. Sears, had it known my situation, would have sent specialists from Mass General. American Express would have demanded a second opinion.

On the telephone, my mother reminded me, perversely, how frightened I had been of the needle. Not just as a baby, but in sixth and seventh grade, when I needed a tetanus booster, how I'd had to be dragged from beneath the examining table. My sons—stitched up, down, and sideways from bike accidents, rock fights, skiing accidents, falls from heights—had put some steel in me. Time had.

And, finally, with sleep coming down fast, near midnight, I made myself think *what if.* And I told myself, without tricking myself (I think), that I was ready for whatever, truly. It came down to a simple question. Did the people I love know I loved them, and were they apt to remember who had loved them? I thought so. If Justin were nine instead of seventeen, oh how I would have bawled that night! I would have known that he'd try and try to recall me, that my likeness would dim, and this would make him feel as though he'd betrayed me, or I'd betrayed him. And then I'd be merely an idea to him.

But Justin knew me, Nicholas did, Priscilla in and out. They'd float without me, and if I died they wouldn't have to live with the strangest story ever told, but with a story that could be told, and explained, and accommodated in a sane scheme. The terrifying part, seeing a standing man tip over, seeing their father fall, and quiver and drool: they'd seen it, and come through it. That night I was kind of the same, but they were not. Whatever happened next would be better than that day at the beach.

After all, here I am, down the road from my valve job. I don't remember the morning hours before they did what they did. Such amnesia, induced chemically or physiologically, is commonplace. I remember waking, and that my wife and boys were there, and that I couldn't talk past the tubes down my throat, and that I wanted to talk. I remember a nurse in intensive care who fed me chips of ice through a whole night, a chip at a time, like a kid feeding an abandoned bird.

They sent my miserable excuse for a valve to pathology. Rhode Island is a teaching hospital, so they will show off what was meant to be paper-thin fluttering valves and was in fact a chunk of calcium with a pinhole. *What do you think this is?* Students will scratch their heads. *Knuckle? Pig's foot?* This way students will learn just how bad it can get before it can get no worse.

I got an easy ride. It was not more fun than a day at the beach—let me be frank—but it was supportable. No nurse addressed me in the first person plural. Morphine rubbed the edge off for a couple of days, and then I went for a week to industrial-strength Tylenol, and then household strength and within a few weeks nothing. For quite some time Priscilla leapt to my croaking pleas for ice water, crossword-puzzle assistance, a little help changing channels, or plumping my pillows. Pretty soon it was "Get it yourself."

Of the get-well cards, I liked best the generic: elephants in doctors' offices and puppies in baskets. Trust Hallmark.

My breastbone is wired and stapled like a packing crate, and they say I'll set off metal detectors in airports. My scar is a beaut. Purple, visible at a good distance. It's not like that show-off LBJ's gall-bladder scar, a twisty chaos, map of Southeast Asia; mine is reasonable, straight as Park Avenue, the cross streets running at right angles—to Madison one way, Lex the other. When I remove my "Life's a Beach" T-shirt, the scar should make an electric impression on suntanners with a few days off from mortality, dreaming of weiners and fried onion rings. Me? I've got a *bad* root-beer twin-stick jones.

I wear a Medic Alert bracelet, engraved with dire warnings. It jangles cheaply, and I can hear my valve tripping seventy-to-the-minute, ticking over like a Baby Ben, or a tuned '56 Chevy, idling. My aorta is carbon and Dacron, simplicity itself, and it's called a St. Jude, after the saint of the impossible, patron of hopeless cases. When I asked my cardiologist how valve manufacturers handle recalls, he said (was that with a smile?) he hadn't really given the matter much thought. ("I'll tell you this," he told me; "I worship at St. Jude's in Pawtucket, and I haven't noticed any dead people manning a picket line in front of the church.") The valve was made not in Korea (or knocked off in Southern Italy, where craftsmen would have misstamped it "arctic value") or worse luck by the Heart Valve Division of General Motors (I'd want to shun models built on Mondays and Fridays). It was fabricated in St. Paul, Minnesota, where they haven't even heard rumors of recreational drugs, and people wash their hands after using the lavatory, and quality control *(I don't like the look of that weld, Sven)* is top-of-the-line. It comes with a lifetime warranty, I'm quite sure.

I think of what happened on the beach and after as training for the future. But some questions I didn't ask. While I was in the land of Nod (they use curare, the stuff little people put on their blow darts), my heart was chilled (frozen?). Okay, where *was* it? What's your hunch? Was it in me, or was it *on another table?* Would that not be a prudent way to work on a pump, as a mechanic might repair a carburetor, on a bench, handy to the tools? What's your best line on this? I could straight-out ask, but I won't. I could ask how much time I bought, but I won't. I've got a more urgent question. Do I ever again have to go to Sint Maarten?

Night Wanderings

JOHN STONE

JOHN STONE is a cardiologist and poet as well as an essayist. His book of essays, *In the Country of the Hearts* (1990), puts him in distinguished company with other physician authors. He lives in Atlanta.

The nest is completely empty now. My two sons are off in Baltimore and Washington, doctoring and politicking. It's the dog and I against the world. As the dachshund snores in his cedar-chip bed in the kitchen, I sleep upstairs. On most nights.

Lately, over the past 10 months, since my wife's sudden illness and death, I've taken to walking in my sleep. I don't remember these night-time treks. But at times, back in the real world, I can partially re-construct what has happened.

I have walked in my sleep on rare occasions in the past, but never this often, over so long a time. Once, in my teens, I woke up my mother by asking her some questions on the whereabouts of a certain "Mar-garet." Margaret was a particularly lovely cheerleader at my high school in Jackson, Mississippi. I have a pretty fair idea of what that little night stroll was all about.

Lately, though, I don't know. When I wake in the morning, there is often evidence of mischief: pictures fallen from the walls and scattered about the bedroom—as though I had been searching vigorously for a door that wasn't there. Once, shortly after my wife was hospitalized, I woke in the morning to find my left knee—and the sheets—bloody. I still have the scar, but no recollection whatsoever of how it came to be.

In one jaunt, I left the hot water running in the bathroom and woke to find little left for my morning shower.

In the most alarming episode, I woke in the middle of the night to find that I was in my son's room, in his bed. In order to get there, I had negotiated the high balcony and the top of a steep set of stairs, opened the door to his room and lain down in his bed. I woke, shivering, to find myself in a strange new twin-size land, pawing the air to find the other half of a king-size bed that had mysteriously shrunk.

Robert Penn Warren, in his poem "Forever O'Clock," speaks of a similar feeling:

> ... when
> You are away on a trip and wake up in some hotel bedroom and
> Do not know where you are and do not know
> Offhand whose breath you do hear
> There beside you.

But, of course, there is no one beside me. I am as alone and disoriented as Rip Van Winkle was after his long and confusing sleep.

Like most physicians, I have a certain hesitation in searching the dispassionate "medical literature" for insights into my own maladies. This is especially true for problems outside my area of expertise, as this sleep disorder is for me. What if I were to learn that the abrupt onset of sleepwalking is often an early sign of a brain tumor? But eventually I did go and ask the reference librarian for her help. She came through with wonderful information that I began to sift with the physician part of my brain.

By definition, sleepwalking is a sequence of complex behaviors that begin (usually) during the first third or so of an otherwise good night's sleep. It turns out to be most common in children, 15 percent of whom sleepwalk at some point. It seems to be much less common, even rare, in adults.

But the true frequency of somnambulism is difficult to be sure about because we walkers don't remember our shuffles. The development of "sleep labs" (in which brain waves, heart rate and other measurements are done during sleep) has helped. Sleepwalking in adults generally appears as a response to stress. With the cataclysmic loss of my wife, I qualify for that diagnosis: we had been married almost 33 years.

Sleep-*talking*, such as I did about Margaret, is apparently pretty uncommon. And the words spoken at such times are often hard to understand. Incidentally, the delightful medical name for talking in one's sleep is *somniloquy*. Done alone, as it most certainly is, I suppose it's a somniloquy soliloquy. Which reminds me of W. H. Auden's definition of a professor as "one who talks in someone else's sleep."

The experts divide sleepwalking into two types. The first consists of passive behavior without attendant fear. For example, one woman removed all her shoes from her closet and lined them up on the windowsill. A medical student who came by my office just now tells me that she used to walk in her sleep when she was a child; she would be discovered by her father in the kitchen setting the table for breakfast or going out at midnight in search of the morning paper. Incidentally, vision seems to be intact in sleepwalkers, so she could have found the paper, had it been there.

In the second type of sleepwalking, self-injury or even violence can occur. Such episodes may begin with a terrified (and terrifying) shriek, accompanied by the rapid heart rate of fear, a kind of "night terror"; the walker will sometimes lash out obliviously and strike the bed partner with the fist. Self-injury is a potential danger, too: in one study, a patient walked out on the window ledge of his apartment, which happened to be on the 35th floor.

Treatment of sleepwalking seems to be highly variable: tranquilizers, anti-depressants, psychotherapy, hypnosis and behavioral therapy have all been tried. So have acupuncture and herbal medicines.

I don't know which is worse, sleepwalking or insomnia. Sleep, of course, is supposed to knit up the raveled sleeve of care, not unravel it further. At least one stays asleep during somnambulism, which leads me to suspect it's the more desirable of these two sleep disorders.

For my part, for now, I've locked the door that leads out of my bedroom, hoping that I'll begin to stay put at night. Also, a friend has lent me a gadget that is battery-operated, hangs from the doorknob and emits a shrill shriek when the doorknob is jostled. I'm not sure whether to try this thing or not. Such an abrupt awakening back to the real world from this country of night-blind staggering might be an extraordinary strain on the psyche, not to mention the heart.

I do think I know what these night wanderings are all about in my own life: they are attempts to do what can't be done in the light—to say things left unsaid that still need to be said; to try somehow to touch, to reckon with, the ghost in every darkness.

Their Malcolm,
My Problem

GERALD EARLY

GERALD EARLY is a writer and editor as well as a lecturer on literary, cultural, and racial topics. His books of essays include *Tuxedo Junction: Essays on American Culture* (1990), *The Culture of Bruising: Essays on Literature and Prize-Fighting* (1991), and *Daughters: On Family and Fatherhood* (1994). He is the director of African and Afro-American Studies at Washington University in St. Louis.

Late one afternoon last spring I sat at home on my couch, disheartened, thumbing through an old copy of *The Autobiography of Malcolm X*. Earlier that afternoon I'd had a lengthy meeting with black students from my university, and although Malcolm X had been in the air on campus for some time—the proliferation of X caps and T-shirts, gossip about the Spike Lee movie, which would open at the end of the year—I suspect it was mostly the passionate and angry tone of the black voices at the meeting that prompted me to pull my copy of the book off the shelf.

I had reread *The Autobiography* many times, having taught it on several occasions. A considerable literary accomplishment, it borrows freely and innovatively from St. Augustine's *Confessions*, the slave narrative tradition, and the bildungsroman tradition of Fielding and Goethe. As a boy I felt it was the only book written expressly for me, a young black American male. But over the years my view changed: the book's rhetoric began to seem awkwardly out of date, and the energy of the man seemed contained in a vision that was as narrow as it was vivid; there was something about the nature of Malcolm's raillery that now left me unprovoked, something about his quest for humanity that left me unmoved.

But as I sat on the couch working my way through the narrative that afternoon, I found much of what I'd been moved by so long ago coming back to me with remarkable force. I read again with revived interest how Malcolm was born in Omaha in 1925, the seventh child of a father who was an itinerant preacher, a fierce follower of Marcus Garvey, and of a mother so lightskinned that she was frequently mistaken for white. When Malcolm was six years old his father was murdered, presumably by white terrorists, because of his black-nationalist beliefs. It is this death, as well as the institutionalization of his mother—who suffered a breakdown as the result of her husband's murder and her struggle to support her family on welfare—that establishes the pattern of both the book and the life as a critique of racism and liberalism. As Malcolm claims angrily, "I am a creation of the Northern white man and of his hypocritical attitude toward the Negro."

After growing up in a detention home in Mason, Michigan, and spending some time in Boston's Roxbury ghetto, living with his half-sister, Malcolm, at age seventeen, settled in Harlem and became a petty hustler and dope pusher. He participated in a string of burglaries of rich white suburban homes but was caught, convicted, and sentenced to ten years in prison. While in jail Malcolm converted to Elijah Muhammad's Nation of Islam, embracing a strict religious but militantly racialist outlook and dedicating himself to telling "the truth about the white man." Once out of prison, Malcolm became Muhammad's most effective minister and proselytizer, attracting adherents and also the attention of the white media. In 1964 Malcolm was excommunicated from the Nation, ostensibly for describing the assassination of John Kennedy as the "chickens coming home to roost." But a schism had been brewing for some time: Muhammad had become increasingly jealous over Malcolm's media attention, Malcolm's stardom, while Malcolm had become disillusioned by Muhammad's extramarital affairs and the older man's reluctance to become more politically active.

After leaving the Nation, Malcolm tried, unsuccessfully, to found two organizations, Muslim Mosque, Inc., and the Organization of Afro-American Unity, the latter patterned after the Organization of African Unity. During the last two years of his life, he traveled extensively in Africa and also made a pilgrimage to Mecca, during which he reconverted to a nonracialist Islam. He was assassinated in Harlem by members of the Nation of Islam in February 1965, just as he was about to give a speech. An angry end to an angry life.

Leafing through *The Autobiography*, I began to see that Malcolm X was the ideological standard of Africanness now being offered up by my students. His singular presence had been much in evidence at that afternoon's meeting. I had agreed to sit down with a coalition of black students—most of whom did not know me—soon after it was announced that I was to become the new director of African and Afro-American studies at my university. In the weeks before we arranged to convene, I had been furiously denounced and publicly pilloried for not being sufficiently Afrocentric to head the department, a charge rather akin to being "not black enough" in the 1960s.

What I found particularly baffling about these attacks was that I do not possess any of the "social tokens" often associated with being "insufficiently black": I do not have a white wife; I have served on most of the university's affirmative-action committees; I am intellectually engaged in the study of black subject matter; I have never publicly criticized any black person connected with the campus during my entire ten-year stay.

But in the eyes of these students, I had failed as a black man. I had never led a protest march or even proposed that one be held. I had never initiated or signed a petition. I had never attended any student meetings that focused on black issues. I had never, in short, done anything deemed heroic. And, for the young, a lack of demonstrable, outsized heroism is a lack of commitment, and a lack of commitment is a sign of having sold out.

Some of this standard teacher-student strife is to be expected; I suppose it is generational. Still, I was deeply pained to have been seen by my black students as someone who compromised, who slouched, who shuffled, someone who had not stood up and been counted, someone who had never done anything heroic for the race.

When my ten-year-old daughter came home from school, she was surprised to find me home, and more surprised to find me visibly upset.

"What's wrong?" she asked.

"The American negro," I began sarcastically, as she made herself a snack, "goes through periodic bouts of dementia when he romantically proclaims himself an African, lost from his brothers and sisters. These tides of benighted nationalism come and go, but this time it seems particularly acute." By now my voice had become strident, my rage nearly out of control.

"Never have I been subjected to more anti-intellectual, protofascistic nonsense than what I have had to endure in the name of Afrocentrism. And this man," I said, waving Malcolm's autobiography, "is the architect of it all, the father of Afrocentrism. This idiot, this fool." I slumped at the kitchen table, placing my forehead against the cool wood.

"But I thought you liked Malcolm X," she said.

Indeed, I was once keenly fond of Malcolm X. I first saw Malcolm on television in 1963, when I was a ten-year-old boy living in Philadelphia; three years later Malcolm, by now dead if not forgotten, left an indelible mark on my life. That year my oldest sister, then a college student, joined the local chapter of the Student Nonviolent Coordinating Committee (SNCC), which at the time was becoming an increasingly Marxist and militant group. Her conversation was now peppered with phrases like "the white power structure," "the man," "black power," and "self-determination for oppressed people." One day she brought home a recorded Malcolm X speech entitled "Message to the Grass Roots."

Hearing it for the first time was a shock and a revelation. I had heard men in barbershops say many of the same things but never in public. I laughed and laughed at Malcolm's oratory, but I felt each word burn with the brightness of a truth that was both utterly new and profoundly familiar. Whenever I had the chance, I would play the record over and over. In a few days I had memorized the entire speech, every word, every turn of phrase, every vocal nuance. I could deliver the speech just as Malcolm had. I never looked at the world in quite the same way again.

During the days of segregation, which continued, de facto, into the sixties, belonging to an all-black institution—anything from a church to a social club to a Boy Scout troop—was like wearing a badge of inferiority. Participation in these groups was not a choice made by blacks but a fiat, decreed by whites, which clearly stated that blacks were not considered, in any way, part of the white world—for most blacks, a world where what happened, mattered. But Malcolm asserted blackness as a source of honor and accomplishment, not degradation and shame.

Within months of the time I first heard Malcolm's "Message to the Grass Roots," I not only had read his autobiography but had listened carefully to other of his speeches, such as "The Ballot or the Bullet" and "Malcolm X on Afro-American History." I had become knowledgeable about the Congo, Patrice Lumumba, the Bandung Conference, and the leadership of the American civil rights movement, topics that were hardly of interest to other boys my age.

Not everyone I knew responded enthusiastically to Malcolm X. I would often hear men in the barbershop making statements like "All that Malcolm X does is talk. In fact, that's what all them Muslims do is talk. Just another nigger hustle." And one day, when I was fourteen, my friend Gary became very angry with me when—with Malcolm X in mind—I called him black.

"Don't call me black, man. I don't like that. I ain't black," he said vehemently.

"We are all black people," I said. "You've been brainwashed by the white man to hate your color. But you're black, and you've got to accept that."

"I said don't call me black," he shouted. "What's wrong with you, anyway? You sound like you been hanging out with them Malcolm X guys. He was a phony just like all the rest of them Muslims. You sound like you snappin' out or something."

I was surprised by Gary's reaction. He was bigger and tougher than I was, and I assumed that he would view Malcolm as a hero, too. But when it became clear he didn't, I felt personally insulted.

"You're black, black, black," I said angrily. "Malcolm X was a great man who tried to free black people. What've you ever done to free black people? You're black and I'll call you black anytime I want to, you dumb nigger."

He hit me so hard in the chest that I fell down in the street, stunned and hurt by the blow.

"Don't call me that," he said, walking away.

It is unlikely that a young black person today would get swatted for defending Malcolm X. In fact, in many ways Malcolm's presence is more deeply felt in the black community now than at any time since his murder. The reasons for his enduring legacy are complex. Malcolm X does not remain an important figure in American cultural history simply because he was a charismatic black nationalist. Hubert H. Harrison, Henry McNeal Turner, Richard B. Moore, Martin Delany, David Walker, Elijah Muhammad, Alexander Crummell, Edward Wilmot Blyden, and Ron Karenga all were charismatic black nationalists of some sort in the nineteenth and twentieth centuries, and none is remembered as a distinct figure except by historians of African-American life and culture.

Malcolm was a fierce debater, a compelling public speaker, and a man of considerable intellectual agility. But, like Martin Luther King, he was hardly an original thinker: American blacks have been hearing some form of black nationalism—Ethiopianism, the back-to-Africa movement, Black Judaism, the Black Moors, Pan-Africanism, the Black Aesthetic, or Afrocentrism—for well over two hundred years. Malcolm's basic idea—a vision of millenarian race-based cultural nationalism culminating in a worldwide race war that would overturn European dominance forever—was, like the Puritanism of Jonathan Edwards, already hoary with age even when it seemed most current. But just as Edwards brilliantly disseminated Calvinist ideas, Malcolm, with valor and wit, popularized ideas about black nationalism, black self-determination, and a universal African identity.

More important, however, than Malcolm's ideas—that is, his popularizing of black nationalism—was, and is, Malcolm the man. His life unfolded like a myth, a heroic tale. He had the imprimatur of both prison (the mark of a revolutionary) and the street (the mark of the proletariat), which lent him authenticity. But, as a Muslim, he was also a firm believer in the bourgeois ideals of diligence, discipline, and entrepreneurship.

Then there was Malcolm's youth. Although generational conflict exists in many societies, it has a long and particularly intense history

for blacks. Each new generation views its elders with suspicion, thinking them failures who compromised and accommodated themselves
in order to survive among the whites. And each generation, in some
way, wishes to free itself from the generation that produced it.

Malcolm's particular brand of youthfulness fed this desire. He embodied a daring and a recklessness that young blacks, especially young
black men, have found compelling. At rallies I attended as a teenager
in the early 1970s, men older than myself would describe the inspiring
experience of having heard Malcolm live. They had, on several occasions a decade earlier, attended Savior's Day rallies, annual Muslim
conventions during which Elijah Muhammad was scheduled to speak.
But Malcolm would always appear on the dais first. He was supposed
to serve, simply, as the warmup act, but for these young men he always
stole the show. While black nationalist and separatist ideas coming
from Elijah Muhammad seemed cranky, cultlike, backwaterish, and
marginal, the same ideas coming from Malcolm seemed revolutionary,
hip, and vibrant.

Malcolm arrived on the scene during the age of Kennedy and King,
the blossoming of youth culture and the coming of rock and roll.
Flaunting his youth as a symbol of masculinity and magnetic power,
he exploited the generation gap among blacks. Because of Malcolm,
the leaders of the civil rights movement were made, through their
comparative conservatism, to seem even older than they were, more
cowardly than they were, bigger sellouts than they were. He referred to
them as "Uncle Toms" or as "Uncles," associating them with the con-
flated popular image of both Uncle Remus and Uncle Tom, fictional
characters created by white writers, aged black men who "loved their
white folks." Malcolm used this language even when talking about
Martin Luther King, who was, in fact, younger than he was. And Malcolm remains forever young, having died at the age of thirty-nine.

He—like the Kennedys and King—died the tragic death of a political martyr.

Malcolm, the dead hero, has grown in stature in our black consciousness even while other living former heroes are forgotten. It is telling to compare the current view of Malcolm with that of another important black figure of the 1960s, Muhammad Ali. Ali and Malcolm are often yoked together in the black mind: two militant Muslims, public troublemakers, disturbers of the peace. But today, those of us who lived through the 1960s return to thinking about Malcolm not simply because of his greater intellect but because we are unnerved by Ali now, by the brain damage he has suffered in the ring, by the way he has aged. Malcolm remains frozen forever in his stern youthfulness, almost immortal, like a saint, while Ali is a mirror of our own aging and mortality, a busted-up, broken-down hero.

No doubt Malcolm's early death contributed to his enduring power for young people today. But it is the existence of *The Autobiography* that has mythologized him forever. If Malcolm—or Alex Haley (who assisted in writing *The Autobiography*) or Malcolm's wife, Betty Shabazz (who is said to have done extensive revisions on Haley's manuscript)—had not written his story, he would have died a negligible curiosity on the American political landscape in much the same way that, say, George Lincoln Rockwell or Father Divine did. Today it is rare to come upon a black student who has not read *The Autobiography of Malcolm X* or will not read it at some point during his or her college career. It has sold more than three million copies and is probably the most commonly taught and most frequently recommended book written by a black American male.

Malcolm, frozen in time, stands before us as the lonely outsider, a kind of bespectacled prince, estranged and embattled, holding a high-noon posture of startling and doomed confrontation. It is this man

who has become for young blacks today the kind of figure that Thoreau, who espoused the overturning of generations and the uselessness
of the elders in *Walden,* was for young whites in the late 1960s.

When I was growing up in the 1960s the goal for blacks was clear:
equality and integration. The civil rights movement, which provided
an arena for heroic political action aimed at destroying segregation,
helped forge this consensus among blacks. Today blacks, confused and
angered by the failure of "the dream," share little agreement about the
future. There is a sense that integration has been halfhearted and has
been achieved only at the expense of black identity.

To today's young, middle-class blacks in particular, Malcolm's es-
pousal of all-blackness—the idea that everything black is inherently
good and that blacks must purge themselves of white "contami-
nants"—may be especially crucial; it is certainly more important than
it was to my generation. These young people have grown up, by and
large, in an integrated world. Most of the black students who attend
the standard prestigious, private, research-oriented university are the
offspring of either black professional parents or a mixed marriage,
have lived most of their lives in mixed or largely white neighborhoods,
and have attended white prep schools or predominantly white public
schools. When they arrive at a university that has an African or Afro-
American studies program, these students expect to find, for the
first time in their lives, an all-black community, one that they have
never experienced in the secular world, a sort of intellectual "nation
within a nation," to borrow W. E. B. Du Bois's term. There they can
be their "true" black selves. Yet in many ways these black students share
fundamentally the same values—a belief in upward mobility and
the rewards of hard work—as the whites who surround them. These
students are wholly neither inside nor outside of the American main-
stream, and they are unsure whether any ideal form of integration

exists. But, like Malcolm, they wish to rid themselves of their feelings of ambiguity, their sense of the precariousness of their belonging. For many of them (and they are not entirely unjustified in feeling this way) integration is the badge of degradation and dishonor, of shame and inferiority, that segregation was for my generation.

I also have felt great shame in the era of integration because, as a student and as a professor, I have taken the money of whites, been paid simply because I was black and was expected to make "black statements" in order to be praised by whites for my Negro-ness. I have felt much as if I were doing what James Baldwin described black domestics in white homes as doing: stealing money and items from whites that the whites expected them to take, wanted them to take, because it reinforced the whites' superiority and our own degradation. Allowing the whites to purchase my "specialness" through affirmative action has seemed not like reparations but like a new form of enslavement.

And I worry about my daughters, wondering whether they are getting too cozy with whites at school and whether they seem too utterly middle class. So much are they protected from any blatant form of racism that I fear they are likely never to understand that it existed and continues to exist today. At these times I feel estranged from my children, knowing that I do not fully understand their experience, nor do they understand mine. For instance, when we moved to an affluent white suburb they clamored for a golden retriever, no doubt because a neighbor down the street had a very attractive one. I adamantly refused to consent, thinking that purchasing a friendly, suburban, sitcom-type dog was another concession to white, middle-class taste. "I don't like dogs," I said childishly before I finally relented.

On occasions like this, when I have wanted to instill in my daughters a sense of "blackness," I tend to trot out a story about my boyhood. It is an anecdote that involves my friend Gary, and it took place about six months after our fight over Malcolm X. Think of my story as the black parent's jeremiad, a warning about the declension of the new generation. And once again Malcolm X seems central to it.

In order to get home from school each day, Gary and I had to walk through an Italian neighborhood. Often during these trips home, several older Italian boys and their Doberman pinschers would chase Gary and me, or a group of us, for several blocks. Once we hit the border of our black Philadelphia neighborhood, around Sixth Street, they would retreat. The Italian boys called this game "chasing the coons" or "spooking the spooks," and it sometimes resulted in a black kid being bitten by one of their dogs. The black kids never fought back; we just ran, later cursing the Italian boys, rhetorically wreaking all manner of vengeance upon them.

On this particular afternoon, both Gary and I had bought sodas and doughnuts, as we usually did, on our way home from school, and we were strolling along when we suddenly heard some voices cry out, "Get those niggers." We turned to see about five or six Italian boys and an unleashed Doberman coming after us. We started running like beings possessed. We were comfortably ahead and easily could have avoided getting caught when Gary abruptly pulled up and caught my arm.

"I'm tired of running from them guys. I ain't running anymore and neither are you."

"Hey, man," I said frantically. "Are you crazy or something? What are we gonna do? Fight em? You must be crazy. I'm getting out of here."

"You ain't going nowhere," he said angrily through his teeth. "It's time we stood up for ourselves. I'm tired of having them white bastards chase me and laugh at me. If they beat us up, well, I guess that's one ass whipping we got to take. But I ain't running."

Gary turned his soda bottle over in his hand like a weapon and I reluctantly did the same. He picked up a brick from the street and I followed; we waited for the Italian boys to catch up. When they did they looked almost bewildered. They stood, perhaps twenty feet from us, slowly comprehending that we were standing our ground. For several moments, except for the growling dog, everyone was silent. Then one of them spoke.

"What you niggers doing walking through our neighborhood? We got a hunting season on jungle bunnies."

"We ain't causing no trouble," Gary said. "We just minding our own business. And if you come another step closer I guarantee I'll put your ass in the hospital."

We all stood for what seemed the longest time, as if frozen in some sort of still life. I was gripping the brick and bottle so hard my hands ached. I felt ready, even eager, to fight, but I was also relieved when I realized we wouldn't have to.

One Italian boy mumbled something about watching ourselves "next time," and they all began to drift off.

As they were retreating, Gary shouted, "And we ain't no niggers. "We're black. Don't ever call us niggers again."

At this I was more than slightly startled, but I was very proud, as if I had made a convert. I recalled at that instant something I had heard Malcolm X say on television, something like, "The so-called Negro has to stop the sit-in, the beg-in, the crawl-in, asking for something that is by rights already his. The so-called Negro has to approach the white man as a man himself." We felt like men, grown-up men, or what we thought grown-up men must feel like when they have been tested and found themselves adequate.

Never once have I told this story in any way that impresses my daughters. My youngest usually says, "Are you finished now, Daddy?"

They know the moral is something to the effect that it is good to be black and that it is something for which we must all stand up. "Yeah," my youngest says, "it's good to be black, but it's better not to have to spend all your time thinking about how good it is to be black."

So here I am, caught between my daughters, who find my race lessons tiresome, and my students, who think me somehow insufficiently black. I need look no farther than Malcolm, old ally and new nemesis, to find the source of this ambiguity. Malcolm embodied contradiction. He preached the importance of Africa, yet he was the most American of men. His autobiography is the quintessential Horatio Alger tale of the self-created individual. Even Malcolm's turn toward Islam, his attempt to embrace something explicitly non-Western, is itself classically American. Americans have long been attracted to the East—in the form of nineteenth-century orientalism, twentieth-century Egyptology, and the current-day popularity, among many middle-class whites, of yoga and Zen Buddhism. Even Afrocentrism itself can be seen as classically American in its urge to romanticize and reinvent the past, much in the way that Jay Gatsby did.

And yet Fitzgerald's novel clearly warns against the temptation to remake the past and the seduction of fraudulent identities. It is in its defining of identity that Malcolm's thinking is uncomfortably rigid and finally false. He developed two distinct but related beliefs about black identity: that blacks are not Americans and that they are really Africans. "We are just as much African today as we were in Africa four hundred years ago, only we are a modern counterpart of it," Malcolm X said at Harvard in 1964. "When you hear a black man playing music, whether it is jazz or Bach, you still hear African music. In everything else we do we still are African in color, feeling, everything. And we will always be that whether we like it or not."

By preaching a romantic reunification with mythological Africa as a way of generating pride and racial unity, Malcolm advocated a single identity for all black people, one that implicitly removed individual distinctions among blacks. In Malcolm's view, individuality is a negligible European creation, while the holy "community"—a creation of the African and other darkskinned peoples—is prized above everything else. The idea of race as community, as invisible church, however, can demand a stifling conformity; its popularity suggests that some aspects of Afrocentrism, or all-blackness, as Malcolm popularized them and as they are preached in some quarters today, far from being imaginative or innovative, are utterly prosaic and philistine in their vision.

Despite the unrealistic romanticism of Malcolm's back-to-Africa preachings, he offers an important message for today's young blacks: that blacks are, indeed, as Du Bois argues, a people of "double-consciousness"; that both blackness and Americanness are real options, each having meaning only when measured against the other. Malcolm would not have argued with such passion and virulence against the validity of any kind of black *American* experience if he did not suspect that assimilation, that *being* American, was truly a rooted desire, if not a fulfilled reality, for most blacks. Yet he also knew that blacks in America cannot think about what their Americanness means without thinking about what it means to be of African descent: the two are inextricably bound together. As the historian Sterling Stuckey has argued, black people did not acquire a sense of what being African was until they came to America. They, like most people who came to this country, achieved their initial sense of identity through their clan— that is, slaves thought of themselves more as members of specific tribes or nations than as "Africans." Slavery compressed the diversity of African experience into one broad African identity, forcing blacks, in turn, to invent a collective sense of an African memory and an African self.

But Africanness is relevant to American blacks today only as a way of helping us understand what it means to be American. While it is necessary that we recognize our African ancestry, and remember that it was, in varying degrees, stripped away by slavery, we must acknowledge, finally, that our story is one of remaking ourselves as Americans. My world is shaped by two indelible ideas: first, that I was once an African, that I grew, generations ago, from that ancestral soil; and, second, that I will never be African again, that I will, like Joseph, not be buried in the soil of my long-ago ancestors.

Malcolm preached the necessity of being African at the complete expense of our American selves, a love of the misty past at the cost of our actual lives, our triumphs, our sufferings in the New World and as modern people. In this way, Malcolm merely increased our anxiety, further fueled our sense of inadequacy, and intensified our self-hatred and feelings of failure by providing us with a ready excuse: America is the white man's country, and the whites don't want you here and will never give you equal citizenship.

But it must always be remembered that our blood is here, our names are here, our fate is here, in a land we helped to invent. By that I have in mind much more than the fact that blacks gave America free labor; other groups have helped build this and other countries for no or for nominal wages. We have given America something far more valuable: we have given her her particular identity, an identity as a country dedicated to diversity, a nation of different peoples living together as one. And no black person should care what the whites want or don't want in the realm of integration. The whites simply must learn to live as committed equals with their former slaves.

Our profound past of being African, which we must never forget, must be balanced by the complex fate of being American, which we can never deny or, worse, evade. For we must accept who and what we are and the forces and conditions that have made us this, not as defeat or triumph, not in shame or with grandiose pride, but as the tangled, strange, yet poignant and immeasurable record of an imperishable human presence.

Selecting a Past

SAM PICKERING

SAM PICKERING is a professor of English at the University of Connecticut and highly regarded as a scholar of children's literature. He has written six books of essays, including *A Continuing Education* (1985), *Still Life* (1990), and *Trespassing* (1994). He lives with his family in Storrs, Connecticut.

My right arm has become weak, and recently I have spent many hours in Boston undergoing tests at Massachusetts General Hospital. As I sat in waiting rooms, the names of diseases spinning through my mind, I realized that I had little control over my future. What choices I might once have made would now be made for me by luck or illness. The realization depressed me, but not for long. If I couldn't control the future I decided, riding the bus back to Willimantic one afternoon, so be it; I would select a past. Besides I was middle-aged, and behind me lay almost fifty years of experiences—experiences like a mountain of marble, not Carrara or Pentelic, but marble seamed by veins of lively imperfection, green, pink, and yellow. From Providence to Danielson I imagined myself a master stonecutter, and the landscape which rolled past my window was not that of Rhode Island and eastern Connecticut but that of Attica and the Apuan Alps.

No man, alas, with a bad arm could ever be a stonecutter, and after arriving in Willimantic and eating a pizza, I stopped considering my past as raw material for a St. Peter's or a Parthenon. I did not, however, stop thinking about selecting a past. In fact I pushed ahead. The sense of a past, I decided, banished insignificance from life, creating the fiction that one was more than just a minute part of long biological and geological processes. A past provided identity, and I began to shape mine, not in Greece or Italy but at home in Storrs. The past one left behind, I soon realized, was more often than not a matter of chance. In the attic, I knew, were boxes stuffed with old clothes, toys, papers, the detritus first of childhood and then more recently, of happy married life. Initially I considered pruning the attic, stripping away branches I did not want to be part of my past and then grafting something green into a trunk to be discovered in the future. Unfortunately I got no closer to the attic than my study. Opening boxes in the attic, I suspected, would upset Vicki and so I kept putting off the chore. Then on the day I finally decided to climb to the attic, the children asked me to help them explore the woods behind Horsebarn Hill.

In walking through the lowlands toward the Fenton River, I recognized flowers: purple trillium, marsh marigold, bluets, wood anemone, Solomon's seal. Later that night I realized that for me the landscape was a flower garden. Because I have never been able to associate names with leaves and barks, I hardly noticed the trees, the most conspicuous part of the woods. Another person would have recognized trees and not flowers. Going to the attic, I suddenly concluded, would probably resemble the day's walk. I would see a few flowers, but no trees, and what pruning I did would be arbitrary. Far better was it to concentrate my energies on things more limited and less strenuous.

Because I knew biographers usually described what their subjects read, I decided people curious about my past would examine my reading. Moreover if the attic were beyond my energies and control, bookshelves in the study were not. By the quick and simple process of shifting books, I could influence how people would read my reading, thereby sketching in part of a past. Most books in my study were ordinary: paperbacks of the happier Victorian novelists Dickens and Trollope and then leatherbound sets of Charles Lever and Bulwer-

Lytton, gifts from friends. Two shelves contained studies of natural history, mostly beginner's guides to birds, flowers, insects, and rocks. Books by essayists filled other shelves: Montaigne, then from the nineteenth century Charles Lamb and William Hazlitt, and from the twentieth century E. B. White, A. J. Liebling, John McPhee, Joseph Epstein, and Edwin Way Teale. Books so conventional would, I decided, have little effect upon a past, and I couldn't imagine drawing conclusions from them. Perhaps someone bent upon interpretation might note the essayists and then searching for frustration speculate about the difference in quality between my reading and writing. But that I decided was pushing conclusion too far. What would influence a past would not be the ordinary books I owned, stretching long in lines around the room, but the few oddities, scattered and dusty at the ends of shelves. So that a past would be convenient I gathered the oddities together.

Given to me as a birthday present twenty years ago by a lively spinster who knew I was interested in eighteenth-century things, the first book I picked up was *ONANIA; or the Heinous Sin of Self-Pollution, And all its frightful Consequences in both SEXES, Considered. With Spiritual and Physical Advise for those, who have already injur'd themselves by this Abominable Practice.* Printed by John Phillips in Boston in 1724 and "Sold at his Shop on the South side of the Town House," *Onania* had enjoyed great popularity in Britain, over fifteen thousand copies of earlier editions, Phillips claimed, having been sold. "SELF-POLLUTION" is, the author explained, "that unnatural Practice, by which Persons of either Sex, may defile their own Bodies, without the Assistance of others, whilst yielding to filthy Imaginations, they endeavour to imitate and procure to themselves that Sensation, which God has order'd to attend the carnal Commerce of the two Sexes, for the Continuance of our Species."

Although he warned "all Masters of Schools" to keep a "strict Eye" over their boys to prevent "the Commission of this vile Sin," the author emphasized that self-pollution was not limited to adolescent males but ran the gauntlet of sexes and ages. The governess of "one of the most eminent Boarding-Schools," he recounted, had surprised one of her scholars "in the very Fact; and who upon Examination confess'd that they very frequently practised it, cum Digitis & Aliis Instrumentis." Although noting that both married and single men practiced "this abominable Sin," the author was particularly hard on females, not simply, as he put it, widows and "Married Women that are Lascivious" but upon pious, proper ladies. Unlike other kinds of "uncleanness" which needed a "Witness," self-pollution could be undertaken alone. "Some lustful Women of Sense," he elaborated, made outward shows of virtue and morality. "In the midst of strong Desires," not only did they reject "disadvantageous Matches" but they also refused to betray "a Weakness to any Man living," preferring instead to abandon themselves to self-pollution.

Onania, the author argued, was the unacknowledged source of many common ailments. In men it brought on Phymesis, Paraphymosis, Stranguries, Priapisms, "Gonorrhaa's," fainting fits, epilepsies, and consumptions. For men who desired heirs it had sad consequences, causing both the "Spermatick Parts" to "become barren as land becomes poor by being over-till'd" and "a Weakness in the *Penis*, and loss of Erection, as if they had been Castrated." Not only did it affect women's complexions, making some pale and others "swarthy and hagged," but it caused "Hysterick Fits," consumption, and barrenness, or if not actual barrenness "a total ineptitute to the Act of Generation it self." Even if people who had recklessly indulged in self-pollution managed to conceive children, such children would not live long, being puny and lingering, "more brought up by Physick than Kitchen diet."

Even more terrible than the physical were the moral consequences of self-pollution. While one could lead only to the grave the other led to Hell, and the author urged readers to discipline the imagination and resist temptation, writing "when Man grows stout and courageous, Satan grows cowardly." Once the barrier that fenced chastity was broken, however, "the enemy to Purity and Holiness makes daily Inroads, and ranges through every Passage of the Conquered Soul."

Besides being a hearty moral tract, *Onania* was a self-help manual, and the author suggested many ways to keep self-pollution beyond arm's length. The best antidote was early marriage, but if marriage were not practical, he urged sufferers to eat sparingly. Particularly to be avoided were beans, peas, and artichokes because, the author wrote, they make "those Parts more turgid." Also banished from the diet was salt meat. "A learned Physician of our own observes," the author explained, "that in Ships which are laden with Salt from Rochel, the Mice breed thrice as fast as in those Ships laden with Merchandize." In bed, men, in particular, were urged to sleep on their sides, not backs "for that heats the Reins, and causes irritations to Lust." Additionally, the author noted, neither men nor women should "handle those Parts at any Time, but when Necessity of Nature requires, for handling of them puffs up, irritates and raises Fleshly Inclinations." If after following all the suggestions regarding diet and domestic habit, a man committed "involuntary POLLUTIONS" in his sleep, the author proposed a fail-safe remedy. "I would advise you," he declared, "whenever you are apprehensive, or in fear of them, to do what Forestus, a noted Physician in his time, lays down, as certain when every thing else has fail'd, which is, to tie a string, when you go to Bed, about your Neck, and the other End of it about the Neck of your *Penis,* which when an Erection happens, will timely awaken you, and put an effectual end to the seminal Emission."

I realized *Onania* could almost single-handedly distort my library and me. In truth I am not the kind of person who for medicinal reasons must sleep on his side and avoid peas and artichokes. My library is a cool place. I think people ought to behave themselves, and I own almost no books in which people misbehave. Long ago I jerked Emma Bovary off the shelf because I didn't want her around radiating heat. The only book I keep which contains warmish parts was written by a friend, and since he visits occasionally I cannot throw it away. I have, however, buried it deep on a damp lower shelf and only dig it up and plant it in the sunshine just before his arrival. One scene in the book does, as the author of *Onania* put it, raise fleshly inclinations, and when my friend's mother-in-law read it, she immediately dropped the book to the floor and kicked it out of the living room, down the hall and out the front door into the snow, after which she called her daughter, shouting into the telephone, "You have married a pervert. Come home."

Lest *Onania* make me seem a pervert or literary peeper, I surrounded it by other, more respectable oddities, cooling it down with leatherbound copies of the *Arminian Magazine,* on the left by the volume for 1787 and on the right by the volume for 1788. I bought the volumes fourteen years ago in London because they contained the autobiography of one of my favorite characters, Silas Told, a friend of John Wesley and an eighteenth-century good Samaritan. Born at the limekilns near the hot wells in Bristol in 1711, Told was the son of a wealthy physician, who, unfortunately being a "great schemer" lost thirty-three hundred pounds in building a wet-dock at Bristol after which he was forced to work as ship's doctor on "a Guinea-man" where in the course of his first voyage he died. At fourteen Told himself was bound apprentice on a ship sailing from Bristol to Jamaica. On the trip the ship was becalmed, and the sailors ran out of food and were forced to drink water alive with maggots. In nine years at sea Told endured worse than maggots, however, suffering through beatings, shipwrecks, pestilential fevers, and service on a slaver captained by a sadist. At twenty-three he escaped the sea becoming first a bricklayer, then a servant, and finally in Wesley's service, head of a charity school. Ultimately, after a second marriage which brought modest means, he devoted his last years to visiting "malefactors in the several prisons in and about" London. He nursed the sick, prayed with debtors in Newgate, and converted the condemned, often riding with them in the cart to the place of execution. Told's charity did not stop with deathbed conversions, and he aided the families of those executed, finding jobs for widows and children. Unlike many spiritual autobiographies, Told's is filled with both the grit of hard living, nights during which forty-one out of eighty slaves suffocated in a "loathsome den," and the grainy surface of cruel justice which condemned one Anderson for stealing cloth worth sixpence to feed his starving family. After talking to Told, however, Anderson embraced the gallows declaring, "This is the happiest day I ever saw in my life! Oh! who could express the joy and peace I now feel! If I could have all the world, I would not wish to live another day!"

The quiet assurance which enabled Told to endure the scorn of turnkeys and persist in helping his fellows did not come easily. Even after meeting Wesley and taking up schoolmastering, he doubted himself. Despondent, he went for a walk early one morning after preaching. Near Ratcliff Row he met a cow. So troubled was he that he wished to be transformed beyond thought into the cow. A little later he noticed a disreputable man some yards away and thought "that man would afford me the greatest happiness I ever before experienced, if he would put an end to so wretched a life." In part because he was depressed Told wandered into a lonesome corner of a field. Once there, a hand struck him on the head whereupon he cried, "Praise God! Praise God!" Looking up he saw the "air and sky, full of the glory of God," after which all became black for a moment. Before opening his eyes again, Told beseeched God to let him know if the event signalled the remission of his sins. Feeling "an unspeakable peace," he dared to look up. Before him the heavens opened into a seam, tapering "away to a point at each end." The center of "this sacred avenue," Told recounted, was "about twelve feet wide, wherein I thought I saw the Lord Jesus, holding up both his hands, from the palms of which the blood seemed to stream down. On this, the flood of tears gushing from my eyes, trickled down my cheeks and I said, 'Lord, it is enough!' From that hour I have not once doubted of my being freely justified."

Our age seems to focus on matters sexual almost to the exclusion of all else, and so I drew a line down the margin beside this part of Told's autobiography and in bold letters wrote "N.B." Still, I wasn't sure it was enough to mortify *Onania*'s fleshiness. Consequently, beside the first volume of the *Arminian Magazine* I put *Lois Dudley Finds Peace,* a tract published in 1923 by the Bible Institute Colportage Association of Chicago and telling the story of an orphan girl's accepting the Lord as her "personal Saviour." Beside the other volume of the *Arminian Magazine* I put T. A. Faulkner's *From the Ball Room to Hell and the Lure of the Dance* (1922). "Tell me, you dancing Christians," Faulkner asked, "how many lost souls have you led to Jesus?" According to Faulkner dance polluted more souls than any other activity, and in chapters typically entitled "Christ at the Ball" and "The Dance and White Slaves," he cited statistical and anecdotal proof. "*Eighty per cent* of the thousands of the denizens of the underworld," he noted, "have been members of some church where dancing was permitted." From California a Catholic priest wrote, saying he had interviewed two hundred girls who were "inmates of the Brothel." "Dancing schools and ballrooms" directly caused the downfall of one hundred and sixty-three of the girls, the priest reported, while "Drink given by parents" ruined twenty, "Willful choice, caused by low wages," ten, and "Abuse and poverty," seven.

Today the lure of interpretation is greater than that of the dance, and I realized someone could conceivably bind the carnal to the spiritual on my bookshelf and thereby reach a conclusion about my past, a conclusion which, like Lois Dudley's peace, would pass "all understanding." In selecting a past, however, one cannot forestall perverse interpretation. After having made "the Outward Shew of Virtue," all I could hope for was that whoever examined my library would do so with an eye less rancorous than that with which the author of *Onania* ogled "lustful Women of Sense." In any case the library constituted but a chapter of my past, and after finishing it I picked up the bigger signature of memory, not initially, though, my own but family memories. On Mother's side of the family, the Ratcliffe side, many people do not marry. Single and singular, they only occasionally approve of each other and almost never approve of outsiders. Just recently, I learned that my great-aunt Betty almost married. When youngish, she fell in love with a man from Pennsylvania, and fleeing family and spinsterhood left Richmond on the evening train, rolling toward Philadelphia and matrimony. She got as far, I was told, as King William or Caroline County, where the train was shunted onto a siding and she was pulled off by relatives armed with virtue and pistols. For his part her lover was encouraged to continue to Philadelphia and advised not to return to Richmond. Finding Virginia courtships a little too passionate, he remained in Philadelphia and married there, not before, however, suing the Ratcliffes for alienation of affection, a suit settled out of court by my grandfather, who, despite not being involved in the railway incident, was the only member of the family at that time with means.

Although the story of Aunt Betty's elopement appeals to me, I wish I knew if it were true. Even if it were, I'm not sure I should include it in my past. One of the problems with selecting a past is that the past is always vital. Not only can it shape perceptions of the moment but it can influence futures. Grandfather Ratcliffe died when I was small, and after his death, Mother often described the things he and I did together. I was, she said, a source of amusement to him. Once while he lay napping in the back parlor, I burst into the room, having tried unsuccessfully to build a toy box. "Big Ga," I shouted, waking him and holding out my hands, "get the axe and chop these arms off. They are no damn good!" Even thinking that such an anecdote could influence a child's development seems perverse, yet I have never been good with my hands. The workings of a hammer, a nail, and a wall are just as mysterious to me as those of a microprocessor. And once or twice over the years, I have thought that if Mother had not told me the story about my hands and the axe I might have tried harder to learn about tools.

What bothers me in the account of Aunt Betty's elopement is the violence. Although family tale has it that my great-great-grandfather Pickering gave up schoolmastering to fight in the Mexican War, eventually becoming a lieutenant colonel, rarely have either the Pickerings or the Ratcliffes been violent. In general we labor to avoid being drawn into conflicts. During the Viet-Nam War when I stopped teaching in order to attend graduate school, my draft classification changed to 1-A. If drafted, I don't know what I would have done. Leaving the country was not something my friends did, and I suspect I would have enlisted in the navy. In any case I didn't face the dilemma. Various universities had awarded me scholarships, including a couple of National Defense Act Fellowships. Gathering the fellowship offers together, I made an appointment to see the clerk of the local draft board. For the appointment I put on my best suit and smoothest manner. After reading through my materials, the clerk turned to me and said, "Mr. Pickering, I cannot tell you what an honor it is to have you registered here."

In thinking about it now, I suppose I should not include this account in my past. It makes me appear smug and cunning when the truth of the matter was that at twenty-five the possibility of my being called up, manners and fellowships aside, was almost nonexistent. Of course by taking word or event out of context, selecting distorts. Years ago when I asked Vicki to marry me, she hesitated, explaining that she did not know whether to marry me or become an ornithologist. To find out she volunteered to work for the Wildfowl Trust at Slimbridge in Gloucestershire. After she flew off to Britain, I thought there was little chance of her roosting quietly in my domestic nest. Three months later Vicki called me. She was in Princeton. "I'm back," she said, "and I'll marry you." "That's great," I answered, "but what brought you home." "Ducks," she said, "ducks shit a lot"—with the inference being, I suppose, that my performance in such matters was somewhat more satisfactory. A decade of affectionate family life and three fledglings later, all inferences seem beside the point, and smacking of a flightier, migrant time, the story has little to do with the woman who moves through my days softer than birdsong. What the story does, however, is underscore the problem raised by time when one selects a past. Mentioning the Viet-Nam War makes the 1960s seem important in my past when actually the sixties like the war did not touch me, not the music, the drugs, the social protests, not even the sexual revolution. I think I read through the sixties, but I am not sure, for never have I had a clear sense of time.

Not just in January but throughout the year I date checks incorrectly. Connecticut Bank and Trust is so used to my mistakes that instead of returning the checks they correct them silently. Of course selecting a past may decrease the importance of time, forcing one to view time not as a series of discrete historical units but as a continuum, a line on which date is less significant than mood. A person finding the initial notes I took for this essay could conclude that I lacked any sense of ordered, historical time. Instead of jotting down ideas as I normally do in a hundred page, eleven-by-nine-inch yellow spiral notebook printed for the "UConn Co-op," I wrote ideas down in a small, four-by-six-and-a-half-inch "Vanderbilt Notebook Student Series," taken by my father to lectures in the 1920's. On the cover Father wrote his name several times in blue ink and then drew scores of whirling attached circles, shaped like slinkies. Inside he jotted down remarks about Thoreau, Emerson, Whitman, Melville, Twain, Lanier, and Poe. His teacher spent much time discussing Puritanism and things southern, and Father's notes referred again and again to H. L. Mencken and Stuart Sherman. For my part I started my notes on a page at the top of which Father had written "For Saturday—a paper" and "Thursday week—a quiz." Underneath he drew an anvil, on the side of which he wrote the first ten letters of the alphabet in capital letters.

I don't mean to imply that time or, better, the times are unimportant in selecting a past. The spirit of the present may actually influence selection more than conditions of time past. I spent childhood summers on my grandfather's farm in Hanover, Virginia. Hanover was rich in country things and country people, both black and white. As the dirt roads wound about between farms, so people's lives twisted together, endlessly supplying matter for stories, some poignant, some gentle, and a good many racist—or perhaps not racist so much as racially aware, for the tales often revealed intimacy and affection. In the late 1940s William, the oldest son of Molly, grandfather's cook, left Virginia for New York where he became a successful undertaker. "Oh,

Miss Katharine, William is doing just fine," Molly answered when Mother asked about him; "he's so light people think he's a spaniel." Mother and Molly were good friends, loving, if not each other, then the world in which they grew up. For years after the farm was sold and we stopped visiting Hanover, they talked on the telephone. I must have heard the story of William's success a score of times, for Mother told it to me after each conversation with Molly. Yet if William were to become part of my past, he would have to be even lighter—whitewashed out of time and beyond offense.

In the class notes he took on Mark Twain, Father wrote, "Dangerous to carry humor too far in dealing with great subjects." Not only does the present force one to shun particular subjects but it also distorts the past by compelling avoidance of certain types of anecdotes. Importance is often equated with solemnity, and the light treatment of any subject, great or small, is dangerous. No matter the selection, if I write humorously, chances are I will have no past, at least not one judged worthy of thought. Consequently, I was tempted to select mostly cosmetic, serious anecdotes for my past, in the process distorting daily life. This weekend I talked on the telephone to Aunt Elizabeth in Richmond. She asked if I remembered going to Uncle Wilbur's office one day when I was eleven or twelve. After learning from the receptionist Mrs. Lane that Uncle Wilbur was busy removing wisdom teeth, I burst into his office and turning to him looked him up and down before saying, "Well, Dr. Ratcliffe, it's good to see you almost sober for a change."

Although I would not want such knowledge to become part of a past, the truth is that for as long as I can remember I have been outspoken. Recently the University of Connecticut condemned four hundred acres of farmland and established a research park, and yesterday in the campus mail I received a letter inviting me to become an associate of the Science and Technology Institute of New England, a consortium of faculty members interested, as a friend put it, in "enhancing earning potentials." Although ostensibly written to the entire university, the letter was really addressed to the science faculty. For some reason that lodged awkwardly in my sensibility, and I telephoned the secretary of the institute. I appreciated his letter, I said, adding that I wanted to become an associate of the institute. The institute, I continued, when he passed on learning that I taught English, would need people to write propaganda and reports. In fact, I stated, I had considerable experience with the legal side of business writing. "Let me give you an example of how I would write a contract for you," I said; "the party of the first part, hereinafter known as greedy sons of bitches, contracts with the party of the second part, hereinafter known as sell your birthright for a dime bastards."

The conversation with the secretary did not last much longer, but walking home, I felt good. That evening I realized my remarks sounded remarkably like something Mother might have said, and I wondered if thinking a person could select a past was only delusion. Maybe a past, even the very words I used, had already been selected for me by heredity. Instead of being free to speak my mind, perhaps I was hung in a groove which had rolled round through generations of minds. Two weeks ago in class I tried to explain how the birth of children changes romance. After the appearance of children, I said, romance lost its dreamy appeal, quickly becoming a practical matter of schedules and consequences. My students were, alas, too young even to want to understand. "Just because of a moment of pleasure," I finally broke out, "just because of a passing thing like chewing Teaberry or Juicy Fruit gum, I haven't slept a night in seven years." What I said was, of course, almost true. Since Francis's birth seven years ago, I haven't spent an undisturbed night. At least once, and more often than not two or three times a night, a child awakens me or I wake on my own and go look at the children to be sure they are still breathing. What was also true was that what I said in class Mother had said to me years earlier in a slightly different way. "Great God!" she exclaimed in exasperation, "because of you I haven't slept a single night in twelve years."

Despite the possibility of heredity's selecting one's past, I want to believe that a person has at least some freedom of choice, in my case freedom enough to distort the past consciously. I do not want my past to have a great influence upon my children's futures, forcing them to live contrary to their inclinations, endlessly measuring themselves against steep, high standards. I don't want my life to weigh them down. Instead I want them to feel superior to me. Superiority brings the freedom to dismiss. And although I hope the children will occasionally remember me lovingly, I nevertheless want them to forget me and live natural, self-assured lives, unburdened by my past. To this end I have distorted my life, selecting a past which reflects a me, often silly and always odd. No person is ever consistent for very long, though, and while selecting a modest dismissible past for myself, I have tried to shape the children's futures.

If my lack of mechanical ability stems from Mother's recounting my desire to have my arms lopped off, then perhaps the tales I tell about the children will influence their lives for the better. To some extent I guess I am selecting pasts for them, pasts, I hope though, of mood not abilities, pasts soft and gentle and smiling. Edward who is five admires "G.I. Joe" and everything military, and although Vicki and I refuse to buy him toy guns, he fashions them out of sticks and Legos. In contrast Eliza who is three likes dolls and is forever having tea parties or staging ballets with them. One afternoon last week Eliza and Edward were playing quietly upstairs until Eliza suddenly appeared crying. "What's wrong, peanut," I said when Eliza came into the study.

"Crystal Star and I were having a party in my room," she sobbed, "and then in came the army." Lest this story someday give Edward a wrong impression of himself, I ought to add that Edward's army is usually composed of peacekeepers. Rarely does he invade tea parties, because he generally walks about the house with my pillow on his head, sucking his left thumb and rubbing the edge of the pillow case between the thumb and index finger of his right hand. Four nights ago while I read him a story in my bed, I asked him to massage my weak arm. "I will Daddy," he said, putting the pillow on his head and beginning to rub the case, "but first I have to fill up with gas at the pillow station." After rubbing the pillow case for ten or fifteen seconds, he started massaging my arm. Because his hand is small, it, evidently, could not hold much gas, having to return to the pillow case and be filled several times.

Under the heading "Things associated with the South by People" Father listed six items in his notebook. The first was Sentiment, about which Father wrote, "Passes too often into Sentimentalism." Part of the southern past sixty years ago, sentimentalism is part of my past today, and I cannot help being sentimental about the children. In fact if I examined the present closely I would probably discover that sentimentalism pervades my days. In contrast to time, particular place matters to me, and when I thought about selecting a place for my past, sentiment influenced me, pushing me toward childhood and the South and away from maturity and Connecticut, a stage of life and a place in which I have been wondrously happy. For a while I thought my place would be Carthage, Tennessee, Father's hometown. I even did research, learning that Grandma Pickering bought her home on November 5, 1909, paying four thousand dollars. She sold it in 1952 for fifteen thousand, five hundred dollars. This past Easter, though, Mother died and was buried in Carthage, and suddenly Carthage seemed a place of losses, both homes and joy. In Connecticut I own almost no land, and after Mother's death I suddenly wanted a place rich with acres and possibilities. Recently I read Teale's *A Naturalist Buys an Old Farm,* and after following him across the hills and streams of Hampton, Connecticut, I returned to Hanover and the Virginia farms of childhood, farms I had roamed like Teale's Trail Wood, observing and naming: Sliding Hill, Red Barn Creek, Piney Woods, The Circle, Bamboo Forest, and Turtle Pond. I remembered the way along old Route 614 from Cabin Hill to Etna Mills: down a long hill and around and over Norman's bridge across the Pamunkey River into King William County. Just on the Hanover side of the bridge was an old house in which gypsies stayed every summer. One August Grandfather took me there and I watched them dance, skirts spinning yellow and red in the green shade. Across the bridge we once stopped so a mother skunk could escort her kits across the road. On the left farther into King William was Hornquarter, a farm Grandfather tried unsuccessfully to buy. At Bleak Hill Fork we turned right, passing Gravatt's Mill Pond and then reaching Etna Mills.

In turning toward childhood for place, I turned toward the past itself, selfishly neglecting both the present and those about me. On sunny weekends my family and I often walk in the woods, down behind the university's barns or through Schoolhouse Brook Park. On the walks I behave much as I did as a child, overturning rocks, digging out the rotten hearts of fallen trees, and wandering off to climb small bluffs or explore marshy lowlands. "Gosh," I said to Vicki last Sunday, "this is great. I don't envy the Weavers scuba diving in Montego Bay." "That," Vicki said after a pause, "that would be fun, too." Although Grandfather Ratcliffe owned twenty-seven hundred acres, his farms seemed small to me, not so much in size, as I now think about it, but in mood and pace. The city's fast pace probably lay behind my not placing my past in Nashville. The elementary school I attended has been torn down, and so much is new in Nashville, even the old, that the place seems to have no past, or at least little sympathy for a past like mine, not crisp Scalamandré roped off in a museum but frayed kitchen oilcloth.

As I want simplicity to be a great part of my place in the past, so my past itself should be simple. In arranging the books in the study, I may have made interpretation needlessly and confusingly complex. With the chest of drawers upstairs I did better, only putting an eighteenth-century Pennsylvania spice box on top. Eighteen inches tall, fifteen wide and twelve deep, the spice box has thirteen drawers, surrounding a keyhole opening. While ginger, nutmeg, and cloves were kept in the drawers, the mortar and pestle for grinding spices probably sat in the opening. When I found the spice box in Mother's attic, it was almost empty, containing needles and thread and three blue buttons. Since putting the box on the chest, I have filled two drawers. In one I put a small silver locket, seven-eighths of an inch in diameter. The locket was given to Vicki's grandmother when she was a student at Welles-ley, and engraved on the back are her initials MFJ and the date 1908. On the front is the orange and black crest of Princeton University. Vicki's father was an undergraduate, and I was a graduate student at Princeton, so the school is part of our family's past, and perhaps like my southern sentimentalism, it will crop up in the future. At least I hope so, and to this end, I put the locket in the spice box as a sort of seed. Someday, maybe the children will find it, and becoming aware of the past, will consider going to Princeton.

On the other hand my family is various, and if attending Prince-ton is part of my past, so is not attending Princeton or for that matter any college. After applying to and being admitted to several schools, Mother refused to go, choosing instead to spend months hunting and riding in Arizona. "I'd had enough school," she said; "books are only part of life." To balance the austere Princeton locket, I put two pieces of Mother's jewelry into the spice box: a heavy gold ring in the middle of which sat an amethyst as big as a tangerine and then a pin shaped like a salamander, its body greenish-blue malachite, its eyes rubies, and diamonds glistening at the tips of its fingers. I had the jewelry because Father insisted I bring it to Connecticut after Mother's death. I stuffed it into the bottom of a handbag, on top of which I crammed four or five purses which Father also asked me to take. At the airport the bag was certain to be inspected, and I envisioned being arrested as a masher or cat burglar. "Well," the woman opening the purse at the airport said, "you certainly have a lot of purses." "Aren't they divine," I answered, inspiration twisting about like a hot salamander; "I never travel without a purse for each outfit. Wait until you get to the bottom of the bag and see my jewelry. It is just scrumptious." "So it is," the woman said looking at me out of the corner of her eye and drawing back. "Just scrumptious," she said, cursorily pushing a purse aside before handing me the bag and adding, "have a nice flight."

I haven't put more family jewelry into the spice box, partly because I'm not sure I can blend the austere and the flamboyant in a way which won't affect my children's futures. Moreover I have almost come to believe in an accidental past, one smacking more of the geological than the rational. The effects of glaciers can be seen all over my part of Connecticut. When the ice melted, glacial drift remained behind. Here in the Eastern Uplands, the drift is till, sediment of all sizes jumbled together: pebbles, stones, clay, and boulders. Whenever I dig in the yard, I hit some kind of rock. Perhaps that, too, is the way of a past. Scraping across then withdrawing from the surface of time, a life leaves till behind, and if someone starts to dig, he's sure to hit something with his shovel. Although I have put nothing more in it than locket, ring, and pin, the spice box has begun to accumulate till: paper clips, pencil nubs, a pearl button, and then mysteriously the buckeye and shark's tooth Mother kept for good luck and which she put in the overnight bag she took with her to the hospital that last time.

Monogamy

STEVEN HARVEY

STEVEN HARVEY is the author of *A Geometry of Lilies: Life and Death in an American Family* (1993). He lives in the North Georgia mountains with his family and teaches English at Young Harris College.

She waves and breaks into a happy run, the whole of her tossing quilted colors on the air. She wears blue-jean shorts with a little cuff at the knee—a skinned knee—and a sailor's cap pulled down over a shock of sunlit hair. A T-shirt flaps against the curves of her body. If she were a little girl, she would leap into my arms but she's not—she's nineteen—so she stops short, pats me on the chest just under the collar, and, bending at the knees, laughs.

"Guess what!" she says, and then tells me the news. Who knows what it is: an A on a test, a phone call from a boy, an acceptance letter from a school. None of that matters now, except her, the fact of her. She stands before me, and we share the planet for a moment—a planet that tilts her like a gem in the light. How could I not take joy in her every time she stepped my way?

Oh, I understand the psychological dynamics of this sort of thing. I'm over forty. She was born twenty-two years after me, within a week of my graduation from college and a month and a day after I got married. The year I started teaching she entered kindergarten. The feelings I have for her are associated with a longing for my lost youth and are, I know, a mask for the fear of my contracted possibilities. My life is a house, doors shutting behind me as I walk through, and now that I'm passing by the room with her bright window in it I hesitate to go on, fearing the click of that door behind me as well.

What strikes me—grips me—is the force of these emotions, their power to consume my otherwise sensible self. The platitudes of rock-and-roll seem profound, and my prose goes greeting-card soft. Long drives are necessary but do no good. I pick things up—quarters, pencils, leaves—hold them briefly to feel their solidity or scruffiness, their reality against my palm, and then open the fingers wide and just let go.

These feelings lay dormant until graduation time. I played my usual distant and avuncular self when she was my student and spent a long time simply trying to recognize what I was feeling. I remember one night we stood beside my car talking about nothing, about school. Classes hadn't started yet, and she had time to kill but no excuse to stay. Finally there was a lull in the talk. Moonlight sifted through the elms like chalk, powdering her arms and hair. Luna moths played around the streetlamp and katydids went crazy in the grass. Near the library we could hear the laughter of students, the call of her world, not mine, floating down the hill beyond us.

She glanced in that direction, about to push herself away from the car, and, at the thought of her leaving, I suddenly felt bereft. "So, what are you taking this quarter?" I said idiotically. I already knew her schedule as well as my own, but the maneuver worked, earning me another two minutes with her. She ticked off classes and hours on her fingers, and I watched as the planet tilted her again, this time toward its lesser light. This is crazy, I remember thinking afterwards as I drove off, windows down on the car, the air blowing past me in a dizzying, exhilarating rush.

I introduced her to some books, works by Plato, for instance, and Kate Chopin and Lao Tzu. She took all to heart and mastered them. When she had a bad night or picked up a poor grade she sometimes came by and cried in the office until I could tease her back to smiles. I talked her through a breakup with one boyfriend and listened with delight to giddy stories as another boy drifted into her life. I showed her *Daisy Miller,* though I didn't need to. She is Daisy Miller, and the book was hers to give to me.

I noticed all that is girlish about her: the whine that worked its way into her voice when she turned ironic, the white of her scalp which showed when she pulled back her hair, her legs—long, athletic, a little lanky—which she folded under her when she sat, the freckles cast along her arms like pennies in a fountain, the skinned knee. In time, though, I saw what at first I had missed: the s-shaped tug that worked into the zipper of her jeans, the sharp turn of her ankles just above the canvas tops of sneakers, the long, slender, tapering fingers of her hands—hints of the woman she had become.

I do not envy her boyfriends—that is the innovation here and a clue that these emotions are not easily pigeonholed. When I see her grab her boyfriend's neck in the dining hall and kiss his hair, I'm pleased by her passions. I want all that for her. She needs a boy, several boys, who will discover the world along with her, not some father figure like me. And yet when we talk I see the beauty of her neck as she looks up and off and my response is not simply paternal. I have to check my hand.

A few days before she left she said good-bye at the gazebo on our campus, and the vague feelings I had for her coalesced, became suddenly as unmistakable as they were ambiguous, and hit me like the knowledge of death. She wanted to thank me for the year and looked away, mumbling "You just don't know." The talk was hard going, and I kept up my end with inanities. I probably asked her what she was taking next fall at the university—no doubt I did.

Finally we got to the boyfriend she had left. I like him very much. He is intelligent, carefree, and simple in his loves. Her leaving hurt and baffled him at once. For months he would show up on campus slumped on porches or under trees like a sack of beans, letting stones and leaves sift through *his* fingers. She spent several months putting up with his long looks and teary eyes, complaining that he followed her around at parties, turning maudlin. She wanted to know why he would not just leave her alone.

"You are a treasure," I said, "and he knows what he's lost." She looked at me. "A treasure," I repeated. She glanced down and when she looked up again she was fighting back tears. We talked a little more, and I remember she tried to say good-bye but couldn't. She gave me a quick hug and ran off, wiping her eyelashes and hiding her face so I couldn't see her cry. By Sunday she was gone, and I woke up the next morning thinking about her. All day I heard doors click behind me.

A part of me—a thoroughly American side attracted to fresh starts and destruction—says do the unthinkable and go for her, sacrifice all for the chase, ply her with sweet words which are all I have, and "give her boyfriends a run." But that is not how I feel about her. It is not how I ever felt about her. I cannot even invent the scene. She would wear a baggy T-shirt, probably, and white shorts—no, jeans—and her hair would be wild and mussy, as usual. She'd have on those goofy, child-pastel sunglasses but take them off when she stepped into . . . into *what?* She would . . . no, I would . . . oh, *it* would. . . .

The page slips through my fingers and rides a lazy, see-saw arc to the floor. The scene has almost no shape in my mind, and whatever shape it assumes turns comic, pathetic, or banal—a violation of the rush of undefinable emotions I do have for her.

One problem, of course, is that she wouldn't have me. A middle-aged teacher would be a terrible mistake for someone who smiles most of the time, cheers with her sorority, and kisses her boyfriend on the neck after class. To her all of this interest on my part would be merely weird. There are other considerations, too—my children, my job. But beyond these simple matters of life and death is an obstacle that dwarfs the rest: I love my wife.

I love Barbara more now than when we first married some twenty years ago. I love her in volleyball shorts, the thighs tapering to a pinch just above the knees. I love the way my shirts hang on her when she works the garden. I love her skin, milky on Saturday mornings in bed. I love to watch her stand on the porch wearing blue jeans and a yellow tank top, and I love, too, the look on her face when she closes one eye and sinks a set shot from the edge of the driveway.

Our love may not move the sun and moon, but it has a history, the adventure of living mixed in. The eyes I kiss—once the bills and laundry and dishes have been shoved aside—have read countless terrible poems by my hand, and the ears I search out with my lips suffered through the songs I wrote and sang back when I wrote and sang songs. Barbara knew me before I knew poetry or bird species. She knew me before I read *Ulysses* or had the who/whom distinction down cold. She kissed me awake on the day my first poem was published and held the hand of my dying grandmother. She knew me before I was me and largely shaped who I am.

Barbara is, without apology, a nurturer. She does not, as Virginia Woolf puts it, see herself in relation to reality except as she stands in relation to others. She does not have, nor does she seem to want, a room of her own, though she often looks out others' windows and rarely complains of the view. In all this she is my teacher—the teacher's teacher—giving a dreamer like me lessons in how to live in a family. "Why don't you take pictures with people in them?" she asked when we first got a camera and I snapped "artistic" photos of mountains, creeks, and storefronts. "Get at least *one* kid in every shot!" Ever since she has been putting kids in the picture for me.

If I handed her shoes to put on the baby she invariably gave one back and pointed to the baby's foot. When I let a baby fall off the change table, she slapped me on the back and said "it could happen to anyone," not letting me off the hook for incompetence. I am among the paternity-disabled but an eager student so the lessons continue. "Get baseball cards," Barbara whispered in my ear last week when Sam came down with the chicken pox on the Fourth of July. Why didn't I think of that? Without her I would float through this family like an idea—a mere word—and would have, in the end, missed all. She grounds me in us, where I belong. With her, word is made flesh.

Fourteen years ago, on the night that my first daughter was born, Barbara and I skirted crescent beaches on the road to the hospital— doing eighty. We passed a lake alive with borrowed light. The predawn glow of cabins on the shore, an anchor lamp, the incandescent moon—all burned a taller, darker twin on water. Headbeams gouged a way into the dark, separate moons on an asphalt horizon, and— fanning a concrete slab—faded in the hospital carport's neon dawn.

In the delivery room, three candy stripers leaned against a wall and observed over the doctor's shoulder. "This is the easy part," Barbara said to the girls, her face dark red and mapped with veins. She had at last reached the stage when she was allowed to push—and did, as hard as she could. One by one, the candy stripers—all youth under their pink masks—slid down the wall and fainted on the floor. None of them saw the doctor put the blood-prize in Barbara's lap, a mystery reserved for those who had left youth behind.

I recall, too, a time when Matt, my oldest son, was reborn before our eyes. At the age of seven he had to submit to anesthesia, and Barbara and I were told to hold him on the table as he came out from under the drug. We watched his faculties return: the limbs moved slowly, as if under water, and the breathing changed from a somnolent monotone to deep gulps after air. The death mask of his face, expressionless and dopey under his mother's kisses and his father's steady gaze, assumed the animation of intelligence. He opened eyes, glazed with unconsciousness, and held one arm out between us, moving his fingers like an infant. "Look," Barbara said, holding now his cheek, now his hand as they came to life, each part of his body filling with purpose as a room at dawn grows familiar in the light. "Oh, look!" With our hands on the awakening flesh of our boy, we saw seven years of maturation recapitulated in moments, and felt the majesty of the life our sharing had created.

Unfortunately, marriage, "with its orgasms estimated in the thousands," as one writer put it, is hardly the stuff of lyric poetry. In memory, the passions of monogamy (that low groan of a word) tend toward the generic. Where after countless nights of lovemaking does sex fall in the memories of husbands and wives, memories so easily displaced by freshly gratified desires?

I remember our first bedroom in a place called The Barn Apartments—pine walls and red curtains. When sunlight filtered in, the room took on a woodsy, autumnal glow, a tinted cellophane beauty bathing us in crimson. Sometimes, in the midst of morning lovemaking, we'd find ourselves just looking at the halo on our skin—our fingers passing through spirit on the way to flesh—and we'd laugh at our iridescence before being swept up by passions which carried the glow to our core.

This was sex at home, our first home. In fact, sex at home is one of the simple, sweet facts of matrimony, which mercifully stops the ugly business of sleeping over at a lover's apartment where one, at least, is not "at home." Sheets take on a soft familiarity when they are "ours," and beds have deeper pockets when sex there is followed by sleep. Lovers rendezvous, assigning themselves to any hastily agreed upon hideaway, but husbands and wives at the point of ecstasy share a homecoming.

We moved to New York, a city so congested it crowded out the weather and drove us into each other's arms. Our building rose some fifteen floors from the concrete of Broadway but remained dwarfed by larger highrises on every side. All we saw from our windows were washed-out stucco walls illuminated by reflected light. When Barbara's body emerged in bed above mine, sheets falling away, it seemed to disappear among the beiges, and I watched the only colors in the room: the splash of red at lips and breasts and the bit of sky—our only sky—in her eyes. All that year our weather happened indoors.

We lived briefly at Martha's Vineyard in a bay-front bungalow with a loft. These were single digs, the kind reserved for wealthy bachelors and steamy, summer romances, but we had the place for the off-season and invaded with our conventional lives of long books and long, long walks. We learned to name birds together that year and tramped over sand dunes with their wavy fringes of sea oats, binoculars in hand, adding ocean birds to our lists. Night or day we could make our way to the loft, no kids to slow us down. Outside the seabirds—heron, tern, and gull—passed by the window offering their monotonous squawks, while our cries, so human and expressive of our shared momentary delight, rang out and dissipated against the swellings of the sea. That summer Barbara conceived our first child.

Since then, we have enjoyed the game of having sex with kids around. What, I wonder, is better than my wife's body in my arms on a Saturday morning with the sound track of a Ninja Turtle video filtering through the walls? She turns to me, all sheets and skin, the light of white walls a cool mother-of-pearl, and runs a finger down my spine. "Heroes," she whispers, "in a half shell."

There is the love scene that hasn't happened yet, but I can imagine it, and the picture does not turn comic, pathetic or banal. All the children but Alice, our youngest, are gone, and she's a high school senior off on her graduation trip. With the kids away, Barbara feels a little blue so I take a blanket off of the bed, grab a bottle of Chianti, and prepare the tree house which like our bodies was built for kids but made for love. I set out candles, the guitar, pillows—the works—and invite her for a walk. When we arrive she gets the picture.

"You jerk," she says—ever the romantic—but before she can protest I've already unbuttoned her blouse. The cat follows us—a new one, I guess—and old Agee, our Argos, is able to hobble down and settle into the leaves at the base of our tree. In the woods, rabbit, coon, and musk-rat curl into knots of fur. A pair of barn owls flutters by and perches in a tree across the creek. Leaves glitter. How wonderful and odd and white and happy are our naked bodies among all this! Even the moon—that voyeur—cannot resist and watches by the light it stole for us.

If I had to pick one time, it would be an autumn morning when Barbara and I were young parents in our late twenties. What is better than lovemaking in the morning, the sunlight giving skin its stub-bornly opaque textures and lusciously translucent colors? Barbara looked particularly radiant that fall, having trimmed down after the birth of our daughter though her breasts were still large and roseate. I ran my hand under them, tickling her a bit. Deeply veined and lumi-nous, they felt hotter than the rest of her and appeared animated from some source beyond us, the springtime of our lives, our youth, here to be squandered daily in nursing. I leaned toward her, tasting the salt in the hollow of her collarbone, and she reached for the headboard, not laughing now, not solemn either, but lost in all that we spend our bodies on. When I held her tight, milk leaked on my chest and min-gled with our sweat in the perfect emblem of marital love.

At graduation, I made my way through the usual sea of black gowns. Eventually I found the student I was looking for and slipped her a note, but we immediately floated apart—drawn away by the tide of the crowd. The note read:

> Words are never enough—that's one of the themes of literature— and I felt the full force of that hard truth the other day in the gazebo when we tried to say good-bye. I'm more than half in love with you—you know that—and, if I were not a very happily married man, I'd give your boyfriends a run. I like your freckles and your skinned knee. Don't grow up too quickly.

Why do we do such things—make such declarations at the risk of being made the fool? Maybe it is a way to say good-bye, but I doubt it because the note was written more to me than to her. It is my flirtation with who I am not, an announcement of this giddy infatuation with what I simply will not be. It, like this essay, indulges the moment to destroy it, the writer, I suppose, growing up just quickly enough.

Drifting in the graduation crowd, I tried to see her one more time while undergoing the customary post-graduation ordeal of shaking hands, giving hugs, and posing for pictures. When I did find her, she was walking toward me, looking bedraggled, but happy, in her loose gown, the open note in her hand. She reached over my shoulder with her arm to give me a hug and kissed my cheek. At last she said good-bye. I am best for her when I am a teacher, guiding her through the world I know and wishing her well in a world that does not include me—that is the truth I came to as she disappeared in a swirl of black robes.

After the graduation crowd had dispersed and it was time to go, I drove off (what cliché should I use?—my head spinning? a lump in my throat?), carrying the present moment like a torn envelope in my lap. When I got home, Barbara—my love past and future, the love I can name—stood in the driveway looking beautiful in jeans and a yellow tank top, shooting baskets with our son.

Inheritance of Horses

JAMES KILGO

JAMES KILGO—author, hunter, and professor of English at the University of Georgia—has written two books of essays: *Deep Enough for Ivorybills* (1988) and *Inheritance of Horses* (1994).

Included in this property at the present time are my horses, and horse
equipment, including harness, saddlery, truck, etc. If my said wife wishes to
make disposition of said livestock by gifts to my children or grandchildren, it
is her property to do with as she pleases.

Last Will and Testament of JAMES P. KILGO, July 1944

I

Jim Kilgo loved a spirited horse and he drove with a heavy foot. You
may think I'm mixing metaphors, but those are literal facts. When he
was fifty-two, his friend Bob Lawton told him to "take things more
quietly, strive for inward peace, make the world your brother, and you
will live to be as old as a cypress tree." But Jim was too revved up. To
me he left his name, five hundred dollars, and an L. C. Smith shotgun
engraved with our initials. Only four at the time, I have been haunted
ever since, longing to recover him, I guess, by gaining a sense of the
man as he was. But how am I to do that? I remember just enough to
know that I knew him, to know that he knew me—too little to go on
but far too much to forget.

Memory begins, we are told, when a child learns to talk, for language is the medium by which sensation imprints itself as image upon

the mind. In one of my earliest memories I am being lifted from behind by the armpits that I might see into a stall where a mare has just foaled. Without a name for what I must have smelled, I recall only the snuffling sounds of the big horse in the darkness and the colt lying small and dark in the dim hay. Another memory from the same period: buggy whip and socket, which means that someone may have spoken that new word—socket—at the instant I discovered how neatly the hole received the handle. I also remember the hearty smell of just-ground cornmeal sliding down a smooth wood chute and dust motes in the sunlight that came through the window of the mill and the warmth of the meal in the barrel when I buried my arms in it up to my elbows. I cannot date these events with precision, but they must have occurred before Christmas of 1944, when I was three and a half years old, because each involves my paternal grandfather, the man I called Pop, and in January of '45 my family moved to New Jersey and I never saw him again.

For at least a year up until that time I was with him almost every day. So you'd think that I'd remember the man as well, the smell of his shaving soap, the rasp of his jaw against my cheek, the tickle of his voice in my ear. But I don't. Photographs merge with stories I heard, causing me to think I do, but in fact only one impression remains. I don't know the year or the season, but the time of day was just after dark. We came in from outside, I in his arms; he took me over to the big desk in the sitting room where he kept a bottle of Jergens lotion, and he rubbed the lotion on our hands, mine small and slippery in his. The part I don't remember was how our clothes must have smelled like horse.

My grandparents' house—an imposing white facade—looked straight down the middle of the street where we lived, one block away. If you walked out in front of our house, you could see all the way up the avenue of oaks to their front door. Here's what I've been told: While I was still an infant, Pop would appear whenever it suited him, day or night, swoop me up from my crib, and take me with him. I was his first grandchild. My mother thinks he considered her and my father too inexperienced to take proper care of a baby, that he really thought that I, like everything else with his name on it, belonged to him. When I had my tonsils out, it was to his house that I was taken to convalesce.

As soon as I could walk, he took me almost every day after work to his horse farm out on the edge of town—a long, white stable sheltered by tall pines, a log smokehouse, and fenced riding rings, where grooms and stable boys exercised his fine saddlebred, and a flock of sheep grazed in the open places. On Sunday afternoons Pop would hitch a horse to his buggy, and with me sandwiched between my grandmother and him we would drive to the park, an undeveloped tract of municipal property of which he had been named commissioner, while a line of automobiles stacked up behind us, honking their horns. At least once he must have taken me up to his gristmill in the next county, for I certainly remember the cornmeal.

And here's what the photographs show: a handsome saddlebred groomed to a high gloss, posing before a white fence with a solemn three-year-old perched on its back. There are a dozen or more like those—different days, different horses—but only one of this: Jim Kilgo mounted, in profile, as erect as a knight in armor.

Just before Christmas of 1944 my father, a lieutenant jg in the navy, received orders to report to a base in New Jersey. He wanted to take us with him—my mother and sister and me—but Pop said no. It was foolish to take Caroline and those babies up north where people were rude and the ground was covered with snow. Though thirty-two years old, my father was still intimidated by Pop, but in this matter he stood his ground. The day after Christmas Pop called my mother aside and told her to talk sense to John; he was acting like a fool, selfish and irresponsible. Whereupon that gentle lady—only twenty-five years old and by temperament unsuited to dissension—told her formidable father-in-law that her place was with her husband, that she would follow him wherever he went, that she trusted him absolutely, and that she was not going to let Pop say those things. She was crying by the time she got that out and Pop was too. They embraced and cried some more. They cried because Pop's other son, Bob, had been fighting in the Pacific since 1942, and because it had been a long time since anyone had heard from my mother's skinny little brother, fighting in the Belgian snow, and because nobody knew where they were sending John. Gaining control of himself, Pop said, "I'm so glad you love my boy."

Some of the people in New Jersey were rude, slamming the door in my mother's face when, with two small children in her arms, she appeared on foot to answer their ad for an apartment, and Pop was right about the snow too. Before that winter was over, I dictated a letter to him in which I told him that I had seen an upside-down house on the beach (my mother added in parentheses that she had no idea what I was talking about), and that I had boots for walking in the snow. The letter he wrote in response has been lost in recent years, but I remember that he said he knew exactly what an upside-down house was. Because he and I were charter members of the Jimmy Club, we understood many things that grown-ups had long since forgotten. And he praised boots. Every man should have a good pair of boots. He had once owned a fine pair for bird hunting, but they had disappeared; he had an idea that my Uncle Bob might know what became of them because he and Pop had the same size foot and Bob liked to hunt birds too.

Germany fell in April, I turned four in June, and my father was discharged from the navy without having been sent overseas. By the first week of July we were packing for home. I'm sure my parents fanned my excitement. We would be seeing Mama and Pop again, and I would soon be big enough to have a horse of my own. I clearly remember my father's disappointment over our having to miss by one day Pop's Second Annual Darlington Horse Show. He had started it the year before, in July, and this one was to be even better. "He's added a hunter class this year," Daddy said.

"What's that?" I asked.

"A hunter is a horse that jumps. Over fences and things."

We spent no more than a night or two in Darlington, which I have no recollection of, and then left for my mother's parents in Greenwood. No sooner had we arrived than a call came from Darlington. Pop had suffered a ruptured appendix; he was going into surgery. My father left immediately.

Pop stood the operation well, recovered quickly, and began to complain about the nurses. "Tell the doctor I'm ready to go," he instructed my father. "Marco [a black employee] can look after me better than these people." But when Daddy went to the hospital the next day, the doctor stopped him in the hall and told him that his father was very sick. Peritonitis. The day after that, Daddy called Greenwood to say that Pop was dead.

As though I were struck dumb by that loss, my memory of the year between the death of my grandfather and my fifth birthday is a strip of overexposed film. I have been told that my parents not only decided against taking me to the funeral, they didn't even tell me the reason for their leaving my sister and me in Greenwood. But I must have seen in the anguish on my father's face that something very bad had happened. That's what my grandmother thought. After I was grown, she told me that when my parents left I stood at the window sobbing for a long time and didn't stop until I fell asleep.

On the first anniversary of Pop's death my uncle Bob Kilgo wrote to his mother describing his feelings upon returning from the Philippines in October of '45; the joy of entering that house after four years of thinking he would never see it again was muted as he stepped into the wide front hall and found it empty of his father, and he wondered for a moment if there was any point in coming home. So it must have seemed to me. I don't know how they explained Pop's absence, the emptiness of my once familiar world, nor whether they ever took me back to the stable. The next thing I knew, they were telling me that Pop's horses had been sold at auction. Our horses. I was angry. With Pop gone, they should have checked with me first. I resented them for lacking the interest (and the money, they said) to maintain the stable until I was old enough to take it over.

The gristmill with its beautiful pond and six hundred and forty acres of woods went to Uncle Bob, who sold it a year later to pay his way through law school. My father took me with him when he and Bob went up to clean out a cabin on the property. A mounted bobcat perched on the mantel above the fireplace. Its eyes burned in that dim room, and I was not convinced it was dead.

The first time I saw my father cry I was in high school. He was going through a stack of old letters and came upon one his father had written to him when he was in college. As he read it, he began to weep. Putting the letter away, he said to me, "My daddy was the greatest man I ever knew."

He had been telling me that since Pop died, illustrating his devotion with stories about Pop's great heart, his generosity and compassion, his fearlessness. "I have seen him get up on a half-broken colt without a second's hesitation. It's a miracle one of those horses didn't kill him." What I heard like a refrain to these stories was how much my grandfather loved me. "He had you on a horse before you could walk," Daddy said. Then he laughed. "You were too young to remember this—you couldn't have been more than three years old—but when Daddy held that first horse show—he was the grand marshal, of course, leading the procession—when he came around to where we were sitting, he stopped the show and had me lift you up to him, and then he paraded around one more time with you in the saddle in front of him."

At the same time I was learning from my parents that God loved me too, that Pop was with Our Father in heaven, that Pop would be proud of me. I knew that Daddy worshipped Pop. He also worshipped God. I saw that every Sunday, Daddy sitting on the aisle end of the front pew where Pop had sat, head bowed in prayer. The day came when I asked my father why he had named me Jimmy instead of John Simpson Kilgo, Jr. "Because I loved my father more than myself," he said. Somehow that answer caused my sense of Pop to coalesce with my idea of God to produce a blurry presence that hovered in sunlit space just beyond the edge of the world, just beyond the grasp of conscious memory. Pop would be with me always. Yet what I continued to feel most keenly was his absence from the house on St. John's Street.

One day when I was seven or eight, while exploring an upstairs storage room, I found leaning against the wall a large board, like a bulletin board, maybe four feet by six; it was festooned with ribbons, crowded and overlapped—ribbons of deep blue and purple, scarlet, white, pale green and yellow, a richness of ribbons and rosettes that proclaimed the beauty of the horses that might have been mine.

Two or three years later I started camping with friends out at Pop's old stable. It was smaller than my half-remembered, glorified impressions, of course—three stalls and a tack room on the front, three stalls and a room with a woodstove on the back—and pines had grown up in the old riding rings. I prowled with a soft foot through the dark interior, careful not to disturb the ghosts of men or horses. Dust lay thick on every surface, and the walls were gauzy with cobwebs, but we found old manure in the stalls, a few mysterious vials of medicine in one of the rooms, and bales of hay in the loft. Unable to summon into memory the place as I knew it must have been, when stable boys led sleek bays and sorrels down the covered passageway, and from somewhere out of sight a stallion announced his intentions to the world, I felt betrayed, victim of a cosmic injustice, as though that stable were the ruined palace of my forefathers and I the disenfranchised prince. If only Pop had lived, I anguished a thousand times, my life would have been blessed with horses.

My father's nature was more like his mother's, steady and somewhat retiring, but I could whip it into a frenzy. The crowd I was running with at sixteen and seventeen was too wild-eyed to suit him; I resented his objections as stuffy and small-minded and chafed against his overbearing authoritarianism. Differences of opinion on topics ranging from church to movies to civil rights often erupted into bitter argument at the supper table. In the heat of battle one day, he said, "You think I'm conservative, you ain't seen nothing. You should have known *my* daddy. If he had lived, the two of you would have clashed on everything."

The truth of that—self-evident and undeniable—struck me like a blow to the midsection. I had already dispensed with God—at least the God of the Methodist church in Darlington; the bond between my father and me was being tested to its limits. And now Pop, who had hovered throughout my childhood like a daily cloud and a nighttime pillar of fire, was suddenly not there. He was on Daddy's side, the third person of a triumvirate of patriarchal authority that did not approve of me.

What kept me from grieving too heavily over the loss was my increasing disapproval of him. As I grew into adulthood, my father's stories of Pop took on an edge—and a darker tone. Even when Daddy meant to praise him, something else asserted itself, wanting to be told. To illustrate Pop's integrity, for example, he said that Pop went to Detroit on business once, and while he was there his bank in Darlington went under, invalidating the check with which he had paid his hotel bill. Immediately, he arranged by telephone to deposit funds in another local bank, but before he returned home, that bank too had closed its doors. Though Pop lost a considerable amount of money in those collapses, he nevertheless found a way to pay the hotel in Detroit. But what was the nature of his business in Detroit? In 1919 Pop had opened one of the first Chevrolet dealerships in South Carolina. In the year the banks failed—probably 1932—the regional office of General Motors sent an auditor around to check the books of local franchises. Pop refused to admit him. It was not that he had anything to hide; he just considered his books his business. When the man insisted, Pop threw him out on the street. Within a week Pop received a letter from Detroit revoking his dealership. Apparently, he had to go north to eat crow.

One of my heroes in high school was our family doctor, Mac Wilcox. My father did not altogether approve of Doctor Mac, at least not as a model for his son, and he told me one day that Pop and Doctor Mac had been bitter enemies. When I asked why, he said that Mac had once brought his car in to have some work done—a car he had bought from Pop—and asked the mechanic if they could let him use a demonstrator. "An entirely reasonable request for a doctor," my father said. "When the mechanic went in to ask, Daddy said, 'Who in the hell does Mac Wilcox think he is that I should have to provide him transportation?' And Mac heard him say it. Needless to say, Mac never bought another car from Daddy, and I don't blame him. That was the kind of fool thing Daddy was capable of, and it hurt him."

Praise of Pop's careful economy might prompt Daddy to tell of the infamous black book, a ledger in which Pop kept scrupulous household accounts; if someone gave my grandmother a hen, say, or even a jar of peach preserves, he would deduct the value of that item from her grocery allowance. "Daddy was too hard on Mama," my father would say. As though that statement had stirred up a sediment that had long lain dormant on the floor of his memory, he would add, "I hate to say it but Daddy could be real ugly at times." Then he would tell of the day Pop came in tired from work to find my grandmother's bridge club in his living room and flew into a rage. Damned if he would have his home turned into a henhouse, he stormed, and he ran the women out.

By then I was more interested in my father's attitude toward Pop than I was in Pop himself. It was easy to conclude that Daddy had long resented his father's harsh authority without being able to admit it, that only now, in middle age, was he having to face that anger. He was doing it by telling stories, and it seemed appropriate somehow that I should be the one he chose to tell them to. In any case, my awareness of my grandfather's darker side coincided with my growing exposure to unredeemed human nature, in me as well as in others. That should have made me more tolerant of his flawed and cracked clay feet, but instead I convicted him of the attitudes I most despised—legalism, bigotry, just plain meanness—and I concluded that he must have been an abrasive son of a bitch, not worth losing sleep over.

Yet I did lose sleep, from a recurring dream in which I arrive after a journey, at a house with many large rooms—not unlike his house in Darlington nor unlike his stable but different from either—and find him there. I don't recognize him at first because I have not expected to find him, but he always knows me, and in that recognition there is laughter and delight and the beatitude of complete satisfaction, all questions answered. Yet waiting for me, every time I awoke, was the stern face in a small gold frame on the table—the face of a man who kept close accounts with the world—and I would feel again the old longing for all that I had lost.

II

I can't remember a time when I didn't know that Pop and my other grandfather, Bob Lawton, whom I called Doc, were good friends. As I grew into an awareness of it, I must have taken it for granted. We *were* all family, weren't we? My father's younger brother—Uncle Bob just home from the war—was Robert Lawton Kilgo, so named by Pop in honor of his friend. When I learned that Pop and Doc had roomed together in college, I still was not surprised. If their children loved each other enough to become my father and mother, I reasoned, then of course Pop and Doc must have known each other in college. When I was older, Daddy told me a story that had become part of our family lore. One morning during their college years Pop came in from class and threw himself rambunctiously upon Doc, who was sitting in a chair whittling. Doc turned his sharp knife upon himself, and the blade entered his navel, puncturing the artery. Blood spurted like water from a garden hose. Drenched red all down the front, Pop rushed out into the street, seeking help. By chance a doctor was passing the house, on his way to his office. He performed surgery immediately, the patient laid out on a table, and saved Doc's life.

Whether Daddy intended it or not, I concluded that Doc had loved Pop so much that he'd turned the knife upon himself rather than stab his friend.

During the years that I knew him, Doc was confined to bed by a chronic gastrointestinal illness that had caused malnutrition and tooth loss, and by the debilitating effects of malaria, and by the periodic onslaught of migraine headache. One problem was always leading to another. At times he was critically ill. Yet through all his suffering—mental anguish as well as physical pain—he maintained a sweetness of spirit that drew people to his bed—strangers as well as friends—from all over the state. As much as he loved to talk, he preferred to listen, focusing full attention on his guest, be it Billy Graham or the yardman next door. His kindness was a balm to hurting people, and his hands were beautiful. As I learned of Pop's irascible, intolerant nature, his bigotry and his pettiness, I found it hard to believe that he and Doc had been so devoted to each other, particularly that Doc had found anything lovable in Jim Kilgo. One day I asked my father what he thought.

Daddy said he didn't know. Two more different men had never lived. And then he told this story.

After he was grown, Daddy had ridden with Pop one day up to the gristmill. There they came upon a tattered old black man gathering fallen sticks for firewood. Pop cussed out the poor old fellow, told him never to set foot on that property again, and then he made him dump the sticks he had gathered.

A man could go to hell for that, I thought.

"Can you imagine what Doc would have said to that?" Daddy asked.

"Did you say anything?"

"My father did not tolerate opposition," Daddy said. "But if anyone could have stood up to him, it would have been Doc."

If a man is known by his friends, then Doc's love speaks well of Pop. Doc rarely spoke of him to me except in terms of general praise. But eventually I acquired their correspondence—the love he spoke to Pop himself, scrawled in an almost illegible script, and Pop's words to him, neatly typed. The letters had lain buried since 1945, in a forgotten drawer in the house on St. John's Street, but they came to light when my parents sold the place, and my father gave them to me—a stack of envelopes simply addressed Jas. P. Kilgo, Darlington, S.C. or Robt. O. Lawton, Greenwood, S.C., each decorated by that violet three-cent Jefferson. I glanced at them, read at them, but, deterred by Doc's cramped hand, I put them away in a drawer of my own.

Years later I brought them out. My father had entered the long, slow decline from which he would never recover, and maybe I wanted to read them while he was still around to answer questions. But something else was going on as well: Having reached the age at which my grandfathers began the correspondence, I almost felt included. In a way, it seemed, they were writing to me.

The first letter, Jim to Bob, is dated 1932, a rough year for a man with a family. Jim at forty-seven was a solid citizen of Darlington—owner of the Chevrolet dealership, park commissioner, Sunday-school teacher, and chairman of the board of stewards at Trinity Methodist Church. Some people thought he resembled Will Rogers, for he had a lock that hung across one side of his forehead and a crooked grin that might remind you of the comedian, but he was not smiling much. A photograph from the period shows a face worn with anxiety and hardened in its resistance to adversity, thinning hair and a jaw gone fleshy. In the depths of the Depression, he was working feverishly to meet expenses, two of which were tuition payments to Wofford and Converse colleges for John and his daughter Mae, and, judging from his letters, he was struggling with his private depression. On a Sunday afternoon in the summer he and his wife Ola drove over to Columbia to see Bob and Anne Lawton. Though too ill to hold a pastorate, Bob was teaching Bible and English literature at Columbia College, receiving practically no salary, scraping by on beans and rice. The visit was a good one for both men. Afterward, Bob, lacking the strength to write, dictated to his daughter Mary a letter to Jim. His response reveals a gloomy state of mind.

Your letter and thoughtfulness were greatly appreciated by me. My wife also thinks it very nice of you to write us, and especially is that lady appreciative of the good judgement of your beautiful daughter [who must have appended a complimentary note of her own]. I am so broken these days in looks and fortune, if not nervously and mentally, that she finds it necessary to make excuses for me. So when anybody comes along and says anything nice about me, to that extent she feels that the burden of a feeble husband is lifted, not from me but from her shoulders.

Your letter though was a real inspiration. I don't know really how I feel these days. Living has been so hard, and meeting ordinary business obligations well nigh impossible with such terrible losses which we have been forced to take over a year or so. Business has never had any attractions for me, other than the attractions it might have for anybody, and they are rather mean. But having cast my lot in that direction rather involuntarily some years ago, I can't do anything else, and though at times I have puffed myself up with the idea that I had performed where others could not have, the achievement is not worth what it cost. . . . I have felt that life, if confined to business, was not worth living.

Clearly, Jim had entered upon some crisis of the mind and spirit. In the same somber mood, he wrote to his son John, who was a senior at Wofford College:

I have always held to the theory that no man can amount to a hill of beans who wants to be popular, who wants to be with the crowd, who thinks no thoughts but the thoughts of the crowd, and who has no ambition or aspiration above the level of the crowd. But this idea, while sound, I am sure, can carry one to the wrong extreme. I am sure in this sense I have erred. I have been rather exclusive in my desires for association, not caring for many people. Not that I have anything against any man or woman, but I haven't the time or taste for them.

Jim's impatience with anything he considered frivolous or trivial and his susceptibility to depression stamped his personality from the beginning. Writing to Bob in 1941, he confessed, "My own childhood was not the happiest thing I ever knew. Somehow I didn't seem to fit into things, and at altogether too early an age I became too serious."

Jim blamed his father for that. The elder Kilgo was a prominent Methodist preacher, known throughout the Conference as "dear old Doctor Jim." But he was anything but dear to his oldest son. Explaining himself to Bob, Jim wrote,

When I grew up I was taught to believe that everything I did was wrong and that children were a kind of necessary evil and responsibility that weighed heavily on their parents, and such a thing as any kind of encouragement to make life seem a bright thing never came to me, except when it could be "slipped" around the corner, probably, by my mother; but then nothing must be said about it. I resented it from the bottom of my soul and was never an hour without the consciousness of this feeling of resentment. In fact, to this day I'm not over it.

By contrast, his devotion to his mother approached adoration. In a letter to John he said, "You were old enough to remember Muddie [the children's name for Jim's mother], and you have always known how passionately your dad loved her." But her understanding of her difficult son could not undo the damage. Taught by a harsh, unloving father that God is the Father of us all, Jim emerged from adolescence miserably yet incorrigibly religious, a rebellious but abject believer in a God he could neither love nor deny, or, more accurately, in a God whose love for him he could not believe because it had not been mediated to him by the one man who had that responsibility.

Such was the boy Bob Lawton met when he transferred to Wofford College in 1903. Years later Jim's college friend Milton Ariail recalled that Jim "was then, as he was throughout his life, dynamic, foursquare, tense and unafraid. . . . His high-strung nature was deeply concentrated. He never sought width but he narrowed his furrow and went deep." The picture of Jim in the class photo confirms Ariail's recollection. On the front row of the stiffly posed junior class, he is the one who stands out, one foot forward, his face turned to the left, leading with his jaw, refusing to blend into the crowd.

He was not the most popular boy on campus. A passage in a letter to Bob, written forty years after their college days, explains why:

Of course you understand my raillery at your wanting to stop at every telephone pole as you walk down a street and meet any jackleg, just as any other pup has a habit of stopping at poles. Or when you find the time to listen to another prate of the values of a good garden site. That all has its place, but personally unless there is something more than a garden spot involved, I have never had the time or disposition to waste my time with such. The bane of my existence used to be getting you from the college as far as Bishop's famous corner. It may have been that telephone poles in the area were thickly set, but it invariably happened that you had to meet a P_____ L_____, or one of similar ilk at every pole, and I had to stand and wait until the two of you had relieved yourselves. Generally the trip to the Bishop's corner consumed about an hour. But that was your way, and I loved you in spite of it, and have never held it against you.

Bob, on the other hand, was loved by everyone who knew him. Frail, studious, and preministerial, he came not from a Methodist parsonage but from an impoverished cotton plantation on the lower Savannah River, the sixth child of a big-talking, hard-drinking father and an aristocratic mother, who, though every inch a lady, was not particularly religious. Except for his brothers, Bob's boyhood companions had been black children, some of them mulattoes sired by men he knew. By the time he arrived at Wofford he had resolved to shun whiskey, cards, profanity, and dancing. Yet his wit and generous spirit so endeared him to his classmates that they elected him president of the senior class.

If friendship develops out of mutual interests, Jim and Bob, in spite of their different personalities, shared enough to keep a conversation going into the early hours of the morning. They were both English majors, passionate about poetry; they loved outdoor sports, especially fishing and quail hunting; and according to comments in Jim's letters, they often sat up late discussing women, specifically, what it would take in a woman to make an ideal wife. But it was not until the summer after Bob's graduation that their friendship intensified into the love that would last until Jim's death. According to Jim's own account, written forty years later, Bob had been on his way through Spartanburg to Glenn Springs, a resort hotel in Spartanburg County owned by the father of the girl Bob would eventually marry. After dinner at the Kilgo home, Jim drove his friend in a buggy the ten miles out to the springs.

> And on that ride, and from that date, I have always counted the beginning of a friendship which to me has meant a great force in my thinking and in my living. I remember a whole lot of things that had been pestering me that I wanted to disgorge, and you I had picked as the victim. And I have never yet stopped disgorging, good, bad, and indifferent. And it was mostly bad, on that occasion. I was really rocked, and rocked sadly, and I could not think of any possibility that it would be of any interest to any other human being, but I decided to put you to the test. That's how it happened. No use telling you what it was all about, if you do not remember. The point is I disgorged, that you put up with it, and that I have loved you with a peculiar kind of love, and felt bound in a way that I had never been bound before, and am still bound in rings of steel that show no wear or breakage.

Such frank expressions of love by one man to another were unusual even in the 1930s, but both Jim and Bob had read Victorian poetry since their school days, and both knew by heart long passages of Alfred, Lord Tennyson's *In Memoriam*, the poet's tribute to his beloved friend Arthur Hallam. In fact, it is likely that their reading of Tennyson provided them with a model for their friendship. In any case, you hear no self-consciousness, and not the slightest hint of discomfort, in their declarations of affection, though often they made a joke of it, as Jim did in his letter about the telephone poles between campus and Bishop's Corner, and as Bob did in this letter to Jim:

You bald-headed scarecrow,

Please without delay ship my pigs. I am entirely against the idea of having them associate longer with you. I do not greatly care to have them corrupted. I want reliable, energetic, serious-minded pigs that have some sort of conception of friendship and obligation, pigs that are ready and willing to travel even a long distance for a friend. It would suit me better if the pigs never saw you again. They may fall under the spell of your fascinating ways at sight. It has been that way with me through the years. People are soon deluded into turning fool about you, and remain so, and more so. That's why I have been so fool about you so long.

To those who knew him and had to live with him every day, Jim was often abrupt and impatient, especially during the years of the Depression, and he could be devastating in his criticism of unsatisfactory performance. But alone in his office on a Sunday afternoon, he spoke to Bob in a tone others were not allowed to hear:

I have loved you long and very deeply. You have been the greatest confidant I ever had. I have had things that wracked me which belonged to me alone, but somehow I always felt better when I had shared them with you. You have been more encouragement to me than any living soul, and I really was that sentimental about you, and wanted your love and confidence so much that at times when I had not recently contacted you, I simply had to sit down to a typewriter and write you that you had to write to me that you loved me. I want you to write to me now if you can. If you can't write much, just write me that I am a great man, even if you have to lie to do it. I like to hear you say you love me because I am worth it, when I have known that I wasn't.

And Bob responded:

You are a great heart, a great spirit, a great man. You hate piffle. You despise hypocrisy. You are strong for reality. You are an authentic hater and certainly you are an authentic lover. There is nothing small about you. None of the elements of littleness. You are a straight and hard shooter but as tender as a very gentle woman. And moreover I am in love with you. No semblance of doubt about that. And I thank God greatly for you.

Though I have enjoyed the fellowship of men and have loved four or five of them as brothers, nothing I have experienced helps me to understand the intensity of Jim Kilgo's love for Bob Lawton. It was passionate and possessive, almost exclusive, and it was abject at times in its dependency. In those ways it was more like a romantic love than a robust friendship, for friendship always has room for others. Jim himself called it "a peculiar kind of love," and when John became engaged to Bob's daughter Caroline, Jim wrote to his friend, "Well, the families are to be bound closer than you and I have been bound, which makes me very happy."

In the cloistered, provincial world of Darlington in the 1920s and '30s, I doubt that Jim had ever encountered a homosexual relationship. If he had, he would have denounced it as a perversion. If any man had been stupid enough to suggest to him that his love for Bob Lawton was sexual, Jim would have knocked him down, or tried to, and while the man was still on the ground, Jim would have informed him that Bob Lawton was incapable of even conceiving of such an abomination. And then he would have hit the man again. I'm pretty sure of that.

What I'm not sure of is how deeply and honestly Jim understood himself. That is not to say that he was a man with unacknowledged homosexual inclinations, whatever those may be, but merely to suggest that his overheated masculinity may have been a pose. Life was nothing but a contest, he said, a glorious battle to be fought by stalwart men, and he was ever hot for the fray. Men less combative he dismissed as "namby-pamby" men such as his father, I suspect. That old preacher has been remembered as a gentle, soft-spoken man, the opposite of his fiery brother John Carlisle Kilgo, Methodist bishop and president of Trinity College. Jim made no secret of his preference for his uncle, and I wonder if all his bluster was just a way of saying to his father, *I am a man now, a real man like Uncle John. If I can't earn your blessing, I will at least get your attention.*

Only with Bob could he be himself, shed the costume, and expose the weaknesses he concealed from the world. He could do that because he believed, simply and without a doubt, that Bob Lawton was the best man he had ever known—the purest, the wisest, the most Christ-like. In Bob's presence nothing less than honesty would do; if Bob could love the real Jim, there must be something to him after all. Listen:

If I had the guts you have, rotten as they are, I'd turn this world up side down. To think of the fight you have made over the years, while you cheated life as your doctor said, and to remember you only as smiling, and throwing chairs at me, and expressing continually the hope that you will be cured eventually, and thinking evil of nobody or anything, but taking the lot of suffering you have been called upon to endure as a heavenly visitation, and believing as you have in a gospel of suffering, without a murmur or complaint, but carrying on in spite of it all, all of this makes of you in deed and in fact an influence for righteousness in some of us who have known you in our humiliation from looking at such an example.

No wonder he craved Bob's approval. And counted it as blessing.

In his last surviving letter to Bob, written five months before his death, Jim spelled out the dynamics of their friendship as he understood it. He was staring sixty in the face. For the first time in his life, all three of his children were gone, young Bob somewhere in the Pacific, and he was not feeling well. On a cold, overcast Sunday afternoon he went down to his office and inserted company stationery into the Underwood. He had not been able to get to Greenwood, he said, because of rationed gas and rubber.

> But I have thought of you. I have wanted to be with you, and to talk with you. Somehow, I feel not only happier, and in better frame of mind, but I also feel that I am a better man after a visit to you.
>
> Did you ever think of the estimate that Christ placed on friendship? Of the test he layed down for friendship? Listen: "Greater love hath no man than this, that he will lay down his life for his friend. Henceforth I call you no longer servants, but friends; for the servant knoweth not what the master doeth; but I have called you friends, *for all things that I have heard of my Father, I have made known unto you.*" I have quoted from memory, but I think it fairly accurate, at least it is accurate in meaning. Recently I had to make a Sunday School talk in which this scripture was a part of the printed text, and again the thinking veered around to you. In the first place, the highest achievement of Christ on earth was to know the Father, his best thinking, his highest aspirations, his holiest impulses, came from the search for the Father, and his happiest moments came as

he understood that Father's will. In other words, it was the best that he (Christ) could think, it was his dearest possession, it was his most sacred living. *All of this I have made known unto you,* and therefore, you are on the plain that I can call a friend. Before that the disciples were servants. Only to those whom we may unburden our hearts, our souls, the best that is in us may we call friends in the sense that he called them friends.

Then he applies the stunning implications of that paragraph to themselves:

I remember on one occasion in Spartanburg, with Uncle John stopped over between trains for about two hours, and in his big, monopolizing way, he talked to the absolute exclusion of [other guests]. When he got ready to go to his train, and told my mother goodbye, she who had sat enthralled and intense during the whole discourse, said, "John I love for you to come to see us, because when you leave I always feel that I know more about God." That was a large saying, Bud, if you can appreciate it. It terribly impressed me at the time, and has never left me, and has been responsible many a time for my thinking on other occasions. Well, those two spirits understood each other, and knew the deeps in the other's nature, so they could be said to be friends. So when you talk of friendship being "a thing of the spirit world," you see that my own thinking cannot be far from yours. The best that is in me belongs to my friend, who will recognize it as my best, and find happiness in the fact that I share it with him.

To the extent that Jim's mother, sitting at the figurative feet of John Kilgo, reminds us of Mary of Bethany at the literal feet of Jesus, Jim not only identified Bob with spiritual authority, but by aligning himself with the women, he acknowledged, if only subconsciously, the female in himself. She was the student, the friend, the recipient of Bob's Christ-like knowledge of the Father, and Jim seemed at peace in that role, recognizing that for all his brandishing of fists, his hurling of challenges into the teeth of the world, it was Bob, physically weak and flat on his back, who was the true fighter, hence the real man. Such moments may have been infrequent, but, as Jim said himself, they brought out the best in him and left him a better man.

Two months after writing that letter, Jim went to see Bob for what turned out to be the last time. After the visit, Bob wrote,

> But here I am running along about myself, when nothing was further from my mind when I took pen to write a line to the *best* friend I have in this world. I, too, had a gorgeous day and a noble fellowship, and your visit was an inspiration and a joy to me. Every time I see you I lament that we do not live in the same town. That would, indeed, be wonderful. We'll have to have it out in heaven. Won't we have a glorious time, Lad?

> I can't get over what a nice time you and I had together. When this war is over, and the boys come home, we must see more of each other.

> But pshaw! I must try to get to sleep. I loved you long ago and since then, and as long as I live.

In the summer of 1941, one year and a week after John Kilgo and Caroline Lawton were married, Caroline gave birth to a son. The baby arrived at three in the morning, in a hospital ten miles from Darlington. John rushed immediately to St. John's Street and woke his mother and father with the news. When daylight came, Jim went down to his office and wrote to Bob. Predictably, he strutted up and down three pages. It was true, he said, that Bob had become a granddad first, but that "was of the petticoat variety." Who couldn't do that? But when it came to "being a real granddad, I put it all over you."

From the way he raved, you would think he had authored the event himself. Incredibly, he teases Bob for being "determined to claim an interest in what Caroline and I have accomplished." What he is really trying to say is that this boy, named for him, is *their* offspring—his and Bob's—in some sense an embodiment of their love for each other.

III

If I could write Jim Kilgo into life, I might be able to recover my inheritance, but how am I to do that without a story to tell? Assemble what he left—photographs, anecdotes, even the letters; add what you know—the house, the stable, the humid summers in Darlington, the room where Doc lay sick; and even so you get nothing but collage, a hodgepodge of nouns and adjectives but not a single verb.

That's all it took—one verb—and my father could not say it. When he tried, it came out in nouns: *that business with that woman.* He was dying, slowly but without much pain, and when I went home to see him, we talked about Pop. I don't remember which of us initiated those conversations, nor do I understand what we had in mind, but I'm sure we both sensed that this would be the last time the three of us came together. Most of what he said I'd heard before, good and bad, but one day he referred in passing to "that business with that woman." He must have thought I knew what he was talking about because he offered no details, and I was afraid to ask, but the verbs he refused to speak galloped through my head.

Of all Pop's flaws, sexual impropriety seemed the least likely. Photographs show the face of a moralist, intolerant and self-righteous—a countenance uncracked by humor, unlikely to flutter hearts. I just could not believe it.

A year later, when my father was no longer even trying to get out of bed, I risked a question. "Did you tell me once that Pop had an affair or did I just imagine that?"

"You must have imagined it," he said. And that was that.

I was baffled. My father, I believe, was constitutionally incapable of telling a lie. If he said he had not told me, that's what he believed. He must have thought I'd heard it elsewhere, but he was not inclined to discuss it.

A few days after his funeral I related that incident to my sister Caroline. Her mouth fell open. Daddy had told her the whole story, she said. She had naturally assumed that he had told me too.

The affair took place while our father was in college, or maybe the year after he graduated. That would have been in 1932 or '33, which was the year Pop's father died, when Pop was forty-eight. The woman was young, perhaps a widow—Caroline wasn't sure—but in any case she was having a hard time financially, and Pop had tried to help her. Daddy had not said how long it lasted, but while it did, they met at the cabin at the millpond—the one with the bobcat on the mantel. Eventually, my grandmother found a note from the woman. (Was she emptying his pockets before taking his suit to the cleaner, or had he, like so many guilty men, carelessly left it out where she would find it?) Devastated, my grandmother called the children together and told them she wanted to divorce their father, a desperate measure at that time and place. They were sympathetic but begged Ola to consider the scandal. From that day until the end of his life Pop slept alone in an upstairs bedroom.

I had known that. Daddy had told me more than once that Pop usually went to bed around midnight but lay awake reading and smoking until four o'clock in the morning, a practice he would not have followed if Ola had been trying to sleep in the bed beside him. Daddy said he'd smoke a pack of cigarettes between supper and the time he went to sleep; every morning the hearth in his room was littered with butts. Now I knew why.

What I don't know—cannot imagine—is how the whole thing started. Everything I've learned about Jim Kilgo convinces me that he was one of those southern gentlemen who confuse romantic idealism with morality, believing that fine moral scruples keep them faithful to their wives when in fact they are too chivalric to go to bed with a woman to whom they cannot commit themselves. That doesn't stop them from becoming emotionally entangled, but they are careful to choose women who are unavailable—too young, too principled, or too married themselves. That way, they can enjoy the anguish of unconsummated passion without risking the consequences. The weakness of that fortress is the protective door—it's locked from the outside. What happens when the woman decides to open it?

It's possible, of course, that I'm wrong, that Jim was just a middle-aged man on the make, but I don't think so. He had never been casual about any relationship, and he was too morally nervous to be casual about sex. He was also vulnerable, as are most men his age, to an attractive younger woman; moreover, he was exhausted, mentally and physically, from working day and night through the darkest year of the Depression; and for the first time in his life he was nobody's son.

Whether one regards the death of one's father as loss or liberation, it is bound to remind him, especially if he is around the half-century mark himself, that his turn is next. I'm not trying to make excuses for my grandfather but to understand how it could have been that he might have said to her one day that he was tired, that he'd love to spend an afternoon by his millpond, get his mind off things, it was such a quiet, peaceful place; he wished she could see it; and she said, show it to me.

It's funny what you remember. I could not have been older than five when Daddy and Uncle Bob took me up to the millpond to clean out the cabin, but I remember, in addition to the bobcat, phonograph records, stacks of them, with red labels, RCA. Whatever the music was, I bet the records were hers, that she brought them to the cabin and cranked the old Victrola while he got a fire going.

I wish I could hear that music, or read the note that must have been sweet enough to incriminate. I wonder if she made him laugh. But all I know for sure is the verb. And its consequences, which throw new light on Jim's letters to Bob, defining and clarifying his need for Bob's acceptance. Listen again:

> I have had things which wracked me which belonged to me alone, but somehow I always felt better when I had shared them with you.
>
> . . . just write me that I am a great man, even if you have to lie to do it. I like to hear you say you love me because I am worth it, when I have known that I wasn't.

According to my mother, John somehow learned of his father's affair before the note came to light; she said it almost killed him. Whether he acted on it or not, she didn't know, but, being young and devoted to his mother, he blamed his father and held it against him. John's anger and disappointment must have broken Jim's heart. In the letter prompted by John's engagement to Caroline, written a few years after the affair, Jim said,

As you have known, John has always been a kind of weakness with me. I have studied the kid from his infancy, and have always tried to establish and keep the most intimate relationship that could exist between a father and son. John is not very communicative, especially when it comes to himself. But I have seen enough of him and his action under circumstances which give me a great deal of pride. I have always felt that he was much finer in texture than his Dad, and still think so. It must be that he gets it from his mother.

Jim's relationship to Ola is harder to understand. As my father once told me, "Daddy was too hard on Mama." At the same time, he kept her on a pedestal, though that in itself may have been a way to avoid the kind of intimacy that characterized the marriage of Bob and Anne. But in that same "engagement letter" Jim's praise of Ola rings with genuine respect:

And when it comes to that subject, as you know I am especially weak. She has always commanded the greatest love and affection I could give, but through the years her grip on me has grown stronger and stronger as my admiration for her many sterling points of character have become more and more outstanding. She has imparted to all of her children a courage, an ambition, and a practical sense of achievement; and along with it she has always stood for the fine, the beautiful, the pure, the lovely, the artistic. Under pressure, her courage does not know a single flinching nerve. I have seen her tried, and she has steadied me. Her combination would be hard to match. So I guess that is why I think as I do of her oldest living son, because I know that he has a great deal of her in him.

In this as in other letters Jim sounds like a man who has learned a hard lesson, but he continued to sleep alone in the upstairs bedroom.

The house was empty in those years, except for the two of them.

He comes in from the stable after dark, washes up, and eats a bite of supper—cold fried chicken from dinner, cold butter beans, which he prefers that way, a glass of buttermilk. If it is summer, the evening is already well advanced by the time he finishes his meal. He and Ola pass a silent hour in the sitting room, she doing handwork, he reading *Little Dorrit*. They are not angry with each other or nursing old grievances. It's just that she is growing so deaf that he can no longer make himself understood easily enough to carry on a conversation. When he tries to tell her something, she says, Don't shout, Mr. Kilgo.

She gets up. She thinks she'll go on to bed. He escorts her to the door, kisses her on the cheek, shouts, Sleep tight.

Then he turns out the lamps and, holding his place in the book with his index finger, climbs the wide staircase in the dimly lit back hall. He can hear her as he climbs, stirring about in the room off to the right.

It's hot upstairs, the dead air cooked all day beneath the tin roof. Because of banks of windows in the outside walls of the room where he sleeps, he calls that room the sleeping porch. The windows have been open all day, but still the room is permeated by the smell of stale tobacco smoke, and not a breath of air is stirring. Crickets and katydids make such a racket that they sound as though they are inside the room. He turns on the bedside lamp, plugs in an oscillating fan anchored heavily on the dresser, aimed at the bed, and undresses—tie, shirt and trousers, which he hangs neatly across the back of a chair.

In underwear and glasses he lies down on top of the sheet, lights a Chesterfield from the pack by the lamp, and opens *Little Dorrit*. The town clock, two blocks away, strikes the hour, eleven o'clock, but he counts the strokes anyway. He has read *Little Dorrit* before, but he never tires of Dickens. In that dark underside of London, he can easily lose himself.

Ola might have him back downstairs now, she's hinted that she might, but he won't ask. He's not ready yet to return to her bed. He doesn't deserve to.

He thinks of the woman, hears her name in his head, and notices his legs, how thin they are, and rubbed clean of hair.

IV

The child who stood at the window crying for his parents to come back and take him home to his grandfather is past fifty now, the house on St. John's Street has long since passed into other hands, and his father is dead. The man is holding a letter—a piece of a letter actually, the first page of the only surviving letter from his grandfather to him. It was written in the fall of 1944 while the boy's father was away in OCS and he and his little sister and their mother were staying at her parents' home in Greenwood. The page is stained and yellow and tearing along the folds. "My dear little Boy," it begins.

> I have been thinking about you all day, and as I promised to write to you, I came to the office after supper tonight so I could write you a letter with the typewriter. It is the same typewriter that you have written so much on, and I have drawn a picture of Pop at the machine. I don't think it is very good of Pop or the typewriter either, but it may help you visualize what I am doing. You can get your Mama to tell you what visualize means. I'm afraid the word imagination would be just as hard for you.

He goes on to say that without the little boy to remind him to check the mail on the way to church that morning he almost forgot to stop at the post office, and when he went through the vestibule, he paid no attention to the bell rope because the little boy who liked to stop and pull it was not there. The rest of the page is devoted to a sermon on good behavior and the importance of being unselfish. Then silence.

I look at the self-portrait he made, to help me "visualize" him, he said. It is drawn in pencil with a light, uncertain hand, pathetically childish. Yet it works, far more effectively than he could have dreamed, for I am looking at it from the Pearl Street sidewalk on a cold Sunday night through the gilt lettering of the showroom window: DARLING-TON MOTOR COMPANY. The door to his office is ajar. The drawn figure at the desk, washed in fluorescent light, begins to breathe. He is fifty-nine years old and feeling every year. That old weakness on his left side has been bothering him again, causing him to snap at Ola—to mistreat her, to be honest—and he is sorry he bullied that new stable boy earlier in the afternoon. He wants to be a better man than he is, he wants friends, he wants to be understood. He pecks at the keys: *My dear Bob.*

I am tempted to knock lightly at the door, confident that he will rec-ognize me the second he sees my face. But there is another page to that letter. I don't know what became of it—it was always missing—but I bet it was all about horses, about how he had one picked out for me, a nice sorrel mare, and it would not be long before I would be old enough to care for her myself, and about how he had been looking for-ward for a long time to the day when we could ride together, side by side down Pine Haven Lane.

I take out a snapshot of him, Jim Kilgo, coming toward the camera on horseback. He is riding in from the left, coming on strong, necktie and hat, the big dark horse sleek with sweat, throwing its head, nostrils flared, plunging against the bit.

Honesty

SYDNEY LEA

SYDNEY LEA—poet, critic, and essayist—is the author of five books of poetry. He was also the founder and, for many years, editor of the *New England Review*. Recently he collected his autobiographical essays in *Hunting the Whole Way Home* (1994).

What is the last book you read? Which movie did you see most recently? Who's your favorite singer? I can't confidently reproduce the
full list of our banal questions, much less what I wrote in response.
And while I remember the two we intended more seriously—what big
change will happen in your life by the time you dig this up? what single
wish would you make right now?—I recall my answer to the latter
alone: *Happiness for my children.*

We buried the time capsule in 1982, during a short campout at Third
Lake. My son, ten years old then, slept under a tent on the sandbeach
with his pal Johnny, my fiancée and I and my daughter Erika, five,
slept in a cabin that had once belonged to dear Creston MacArthur,
for whom the son was named.

Though now, the decade flown and more, Erika writes like an angel
herself, that August she was still mystified by the written word. She
needed help, and she got it from the woman who'd soon be her step-
mother. I recall how annoying she found such dependence; hers would
be the only answers known to another person. Yet the little girl's un-
happiness seemed nothing beside her brother's rage and pain, his far
more embittering mystification. How in God's name, after all, could

his flesh-and-blood father mean to marry a different woman from his flesh-and-blood mother?

Yet it was not only for domestic reasons that I found our stay hard. Some of the best moments of my younger life had transpired on this very spot—and had come to a heartbreaking halt with Creston MacArthur's death in 1976. Six short years, but such a lot of water over the dam! Even today the platitude seems right as I think of Third Lake, the rivermen driving their booms out of it and down the Machias.

A son of summer folks, of course, I never saw the drive—except inwardly, through the visions that Creston and others planted in my mind. Pickpoles. Rough women waiting at the bridges. Some bare-knuckle flareup over a stolen whetstone. Cream of Tartar biscuits and beans four times each day. Arthur, the Passamaquoddy who always set the dynamite charge to break a jam, who "trotted them logs like a mink would," as one old river hand put it.

When I first heard such particulars, they struck me with an almost frightening vividness; I needed actual force of will to remember I'd not made that run myself, and even now—less susceptible to such delusion—I remain stirred by the scenes I once imagined, and will forever.

The oldtimers let a big head build, then opened the gates, everything racing seaward in a mass.

There's a small marsh—or heath, as the Scots-derived natives say—not far upshore from the Third Lake cabin. Creston and I watched that wetland in many a summer's dusk, just to see what would walk into it, or fly: cow moose liked the place, despite its mosquitoes and gadflies, though for some reason no grown bull ever showed there; it was a favorite too of mergansers, who'd scrabble after the plentiful frogs, churning dark mud till we smelled it even from our distance; deer drank from the red water pooled on the heath's inland edge, just under boughs of crowding cedar.

But things were different in the summer of the owl. He would drop from a hemlock behind the cabin, drifting in his absolute, uncanny silence over our heads, cruising the cattails and grasses of the marsh, low as a harrier, at last flinging up a wing and banking sharply earthward and taking flight again—all one motion—with an indistinguishable small something in his grip.

Inside that deep plumage, the great horned owl is actually dove-sized. Deadly though he be, then, he'll not take on a big duck. And yet the August I speak of was a month of no mergansers. Even the moose and deer stayed absent. We'd see nothing but dusk's fierce raptor, who worried the amphibians and rodents to literal death, for he never rose from that slue empty-clawed.

"Find me a man that hunts like that," Creston mused one evening, "and I'll stove his gun for him."

I could not see the man's big grin, backlit as he was by the last of sunlight, but I remember somehow *feeling* it like the sudden breeze that kicked up, bending the marshweeds our way, ferrying the smell to us of the heath, a rankness I still inhale like perfume: smell of a bird dog after a hardworking day, of a duck blind at dawn, of a mudbar where the river slowly eddies and big trout sip from the backwash, challenging a cast's precision. It speaks of a world ever shrinking, the one not yet locked under asphalt.

Once the owl's lethal patrol was finished, I remember how abruptly the sun tumbled, the way it does in a place with lots of sky and a ridgey horizon. If we'd worn any, we could have set our watches by the bird, whose rite was constant night after night, or at least seemed so whenever we came into camp—as it turned out we'd never do again, not in each other's company.

Since the summer of our owl, I have returned three times to the Third Lake camp.

In October of '76, eight months after Creston's death, I went out alone, meaning to do some jumpshooting in Mutton Cove and Dead Stream and along the shallow north shore of the Middleground, the same spots in which we'd so often scouted ducks together. But there seemed omens everywhere, and they distracted me, above all and unaccountably an old-fashioned hightop Ked sneaker, its lace strung to Creston's clothesline. I remember wondering what on earth he could have used *that* for, and when. It wasn't simple bafflement, though, that kept me sleepless. Sometime during the small hours, I watched a squall rush from the Machias dam across to the campyard, and in its unseasonable flashes of lightning I beheld the wind-driven shoe, wheeling in ragged orbit, the sight of it flooding me with unnameable fear, and a sadness weighty as iron.

I had three days to spare, and come dawn I found ducks enough as ordinarily to keep me interested for the full of that time. Yet I paddled out before noontime, shivering in a rain that had turned to quiet, frigid drizzle. In the bow my retriever shivered too, his face so dark and mournful I dreamed he knew my grief.

The Ked still hung there on my next trip, in that August of '82 when we hid our capsule. Though by now it had a different aspect, the winters having changed it from black to ghostly, it continued oddly to oppress me, and during the first afternoon—while the rest were swimming—I walked to the clothesline, open jackknife in hand. And yet somehow I couldn't cut that icon down.

On the following day we turned to our questionnaire. When we had finished, we put our papers in a sealable plastic bag. Next we stuck that bag in a small coffee can, which we wrapped in yet a bigger plastic bag. Then we deposited the smaller can in a larger, and finally swaddled the whole works in a big green leaf sack.

We decided to make our hole just west of Creston's cabin, where the sandbeach comes to a point. A great pyramid stone stands there, well above high water line, so that the rock marked a good, dry site. The digging was easy, fun: even Erika took a hand in it.

My third visit came in 1992, ten years later. Though the decade passed with dizzying speed, Georgia Pacific managed in that short span to carve more roads in the back country than one would have thought feasible. One of these ran to the Third Lake shore not far from where our capsule lay buried. I drove it, muttering the whole way, passing the murderous chipping operations, the clearcuts with their trompe l'oeil facades of reseeded growth on the shoulders. To approach that water by car and not canoe didn't feel right in the first place. It was shameful of me to accede to the convenience of a road—the kind of convenience that's ruining wildness all over the world.

Yet what canoe would hold us all now? My son Creston, six feet six inches tall, was spending the summer doing research for his favorite college professor. His friend Johnny, a U.S. Marine now, was off in some barracks. But my daughter Erika was with us again, along with the three small siblings who'd been born since '82, one of them a six-month-old baby girl with her father's androgynous name. We'd brought my twin twelve-year-old nieces for good measure, making an outing of it—some swimming, exploring, food. After all, only Erika and Robin and I had been present at the capsule's interment, and of these I'd been the single one to have known Creston MacArthur as more than a name.

We finally fetched up at lakeside. A gigantic A-frame, surrounded by all-terrain vehicles, stood there, strange as cancer. I knocked on the door, but no one responded. Stepping over to the bluff, I looked down on a row of aluminum motorboats. A plastic soda bottle and two Bud empties rolled back and forth in the rote; but no one was down there either.

When I went back to the car, our gang spilled out. I pointed west along the shore. "Just walk that way a few hundred yards," I said. The kids took off like hounds, all but little Sydney, whom I loaded into a carrying pack.

Grabbing the spade, I stood in my tracks for a moment, facing away from my car, from the new building, from the ranks of three-wheelers and powerboats. I could make out the owl's marsh in the near distance; somebody had driven a post in its middle and strung a cable from there up to the knoll where I stood. I guessed the rig was for one of those running deer effigies: you let the thing slide on its wire and then shoot. You aim behind the metal foreshoulder at the sham heart.

The baby fell quickly asleep on my back. Strolling downhill to where the high tier flattens and joins the beach, I stopped again, wanting to give the others a generous head start, wanting to walk that edge alone, slow and speechless. Or maybe not to walk it at all.

On my desk at home I have a photograph of Creston, his canoe nosed ashore just at that spot. Wearing a green-plaid mackinaw and a hueless baseball cap, he sits in the stern. His hands are raised, and he sights along an imaginary shotgun. The picture catches him in the midst of one of his countless hunting tales—I can't remember which, and it doesn't matter: it fills me with joy and melancholy anyhow.

Cross lake, I noticed a soaring bird. An eagle, I imagined, but when I squinted it turned into a gull, its squawks borne my way by the south wind. That blow bore weather too. The day, which had started bright, was graying fast, and the change made me think of another time many years gone, over there on the Middleground.

I'd come out with Creston's uncle George MacArthur. I called him uncle too. Each of us, unbeknownst to the other, had brought a fifth of whiskey, and we lay on the beach till midnight, trading talk and song, drinking his jug down to empty. And then, fools that we were, we drank down mine. We lolled there till dawn, which broke into south wind like this. And then came the piddling rain.

A boy, I could handle such hours of carousing, though they'd maybe kill me today. George was in his seventies, and on the trip home he swore they damn near did kill him. I can still see him in the bow of our boat, a short but huge-shouldered man, his whole frame slouching. Every fifth stroke or so he points his paddle toward the sky, letting lake water run down the shaft and into his parched mouth.

And yet forever after George would claim that that misery had been worth it—for the time we had on our trip, for the things we sang and said, which I'll bet were among the best ever to pass between us. The words have flown from memory; indeed, most of them were likely gone by morning; but the conversation counted much less in any case than the fact that we held it where names of land- and watermarks provided all the eloquence anyone could need: Freeze-to-Death Island, the Burn, Washington Bald Mountain, Slaughter Point. Who cared about our talk's specific content?

Yet even back then was I not a man for content? I believed a writer's job was to take the impressions of a time and setting and to recall or invent their specifics, to give them back the voices that had fallen mute or that never existed in the first place.

Today I smile ruefully at certain of my old naivetés. I quickly learned, for example, that there's no such thing as the voice of nature or even of place—or none at least that will yield to human translation. And yet there did remain the voices of *people* whose lives were drenched in the natural. Years ago, maybe during the course of that very liquory night with George, I surmised that I might render the rhythms and cadences of those voices without having to imitate them exactly. That it would in any case be worth finding out.

Hearing a faint flat vowel over the breeze, I reeled my mind back to now, to 1992: down the lakeshore, I could see small figures waving towels and bits of clothing; what I'd heard was likely the *a* in "Dad," the children calling to me, who held the shovel. How long must I have been stuck in my reverie, oblivious even of the baby on my back?

To travel toward the point was another act of will, for I couldn't cover ten yards of beach without coming on something to stop me again in my tracks. Will, however, prevailed.

Until I came in sight of the campyard.

Just over there lay the rocks Creston and I used to sit on as we scanned our marsh. Our moose. Our deer. Our sheldrakes gigging blackback frogs. Our owl, so lethal, quiet, punctual. There too stood the outdoor fireplace, where we broiled two duck one October evening. Oh, we cooked plenty of others over such a blaze, but that pair proved somehow the best of the many, probably because we ate them just after the finest duck-hunting day of my life.

Uphill, tucked just under the hemlock canopy, was the cabin itself, timbers fitted on the vertical: when a man builds a camp all alone he can't handle a long log on the horizontal; he makes a sill, then balances an end of his stick on it with one hand and hammers with the other— a tricky, tentative business. Everything can fall down on you before you know it.

The lowness of the doorway; the faded verdigris oakum chinking the walls; the beachstone chimney; the sagging wharf from which loud children were jumping now into water; the rotted outdoor table; an axe still lying on the porch, its handle fretted by porcupines who craved the dead man's traces of sweat.

Physical particulars damn near undid me. I huffed suddenly, uncontrollably, exactly as I have done each time I've seen a child burst out of the womb.

"What's the matter?" It was Erika.

"Oh, a lot of memories," I whispered, forcing a self-dismissive grin.

My wife kissed me on the cheek and rubbed my shoulders. Her imagination has always equaled my own, at least.

For all the moment's pathos, Robin's kindness reminded me that I was a lucky man, and had always been, in so many ways. By this very lake, for example, I'd once decided to be a writer; and now something was all but writing itself as I stood again on its shore. There weren't many, I guessed, who could walk just so into a waiting metaphorical scheme: the past unburying itself.

That scheme, however, was soon skewed. I dug so wide and so deep around our rock that at last I feared it might fall in upon me. But I could not find our time capsule.

At length I flung myself on the sand, exhausted not so much from physical effort as self-contempt. How like me, this fiasco! How often had I discovered a new bird cover, for example, and then—all eagerness to hunt it—subsequently forgotten the roads I'd taken to get there? How many days had I spent in searches, sometimes vain, to rediscover places? How often had I vowed to notice the world more carefully?

Yet here I was, so sure I knew the paths I'd followed—so profoundly wrong again. And if one memory could fail me like this, what faith might I put in other memories? Perhaps the past could never *be* exhumed. That was a dispiriting thought for an elegist, enough so that I imagined laying all the pages I'd ever written end to end along this beach. They'd reach a considerable distance, well past the owl's heath. If I waited till the wind swung west again, I could touch a match to the first sheet, then watch the flame run back, against the way I'd come.

Except in my very occasional forays into fiction, I have always felt an obligation to factual truth in my writing, to honesty in that sense. There is nothing moralistic in such a feeling; it is only that I find it enabling. Standing on that particular lakeshore, before my dead friend's camp, I felt that enablement buckle.

Earlier in the afternoon, for instance, I'd remembered a certain day of duck-hunting as the finest in my life, but in what, I now wondered, did its fineness consist? The two birds we broiled over the old fireplace may have tasted as wonderful as they did primarily because they were the only spoils from a miserably uncomfortable trip: I learned among other things why Freeze-to-Death Island had gotten its name, stationed there while Creston jumped a black-duck raft in Mutton cove, all the birds spooking before he could get within range, and none flying over that cold clump of rocks where I huddled. Then I tried my unsuccessful hand at sneaking on a flock, this one rafted in the Eastern Arm, while Creston hid in the high-bush blueberries on the bank of Dead Stream. He never fired a shot.

Toward dusk we crippled a whistler, but though my Labrador

searched for a long, long time, it got away, went off somewhere to die in pain, alone.

I remembered that just before bedtime we drank a toddy—bourbon, hot water, and sugar. How good, how warming it seemed. And how badly I wanted more, wanted, say, the two full bottles that Uncle George and I had consumed that night on the Middleground. Since I was onto issues of honesty, it seemed worth recalling that that trip might well have marked an early chapter in the dazing subsequent years of my battle with booze.

And booze, having done well to break up my first marriage, in some measure engendered the feelings my firstborn had tried and failed to contain when we buried that time capsule in 1982: pain, anger, pure mystification. Supposing we *had* found the buried writings: what might they have said about the past, and how much pleasure might I take in it? I didn't need to tax myself much to imagine the sort of thing that that firstborn boy had recorded as his biggest wish: for my fiancée to crawl into Third Lake and become a white perch, a turtle, a polliwog—anything but what she was.

My own big wish, for my children to be happy, extended perhaps above all to that son Creston, for I knew how far out of reach such a prospect seemed in 1982. However brilliantly he now fares, back then it must have seemed as though someone had died, a death as tragic to him as that other Creston's to me.

Lying next to that large gap in the sand, yet another line from Emily Dickinson occurred to me: "Tell all the truth, but tell it slant." Maybe, I thought, that's what I've been doing for a long time. It was a hopeful notion, according to which my bittersweet recalls of a George or Creston MacArthur, those voices murmuring in the unspecific half-light, might be truth purged of its nagging contradictions.

And yet the more sobering possibility remained that I could mention nothing with certainty beyond the names of such men, the names of some other persons, and certain indelible facts, however plain: an owl; a cabin; a lake; an island or two; a basketball shoe wheeling crazily on its lace. I could be honest at least about the likes of these, and to such likes must I even now repair—again and again—as I dig up the past, or try.